EPIC FAIL
super win

27 CANDID INTERVIEWS ON FAILURE & SUCCESS

WITH CREATIVE PEOPLE
WHO KEPT GOING

CURATED BY SERENA ANDREWS

2014 | Dream Siren | New York, NY

Copyright

First Printing: 2014

ISBN 978-1-304-75397-7

Dream Siren
New York, NY

Dedication

Dedicated to all the generous people who helped fund and support my Indiegogo campaign to make this book and the tour surrounding it happen.

Thank you deeply.

Table Of Contents

Professor Cyclone

My friend Amèlie and I went on a trip to Coney Island earlier this summer. At the time, I was thinking a lot about polarity versus rhythm. It's funny how the mind works. As soon as you begin to focus thoughts on a particular thing or idea, suddenly you see it everywhere.

Say what you want, I felt that the universe itself was speaking to me through this beachside amusement park! We were out all day, until it got dark. We spent about half the day near the water watching the waves. Then we tackled the rides–about four roller coasters including my favorite, The Cyclone. Finally we got dinner and headed home. With each piece of our day there were perfect examples of polarity and rhythm. Everything one really needs to know about these concepts can be learned by observing physics as it happens in nature, or through practical application... especially at a Coney Island!

~

It is day into night, low tide into high, hunger to a satisfied belly, heights plunging to depths, waves ebbing, fear of an experience matched by the courage to test it.

Failure and Success.

Intrinsically, there can never be the one side without its opposite and usually one follows the other in a rhythm.

We heart superlatives.

If you really think about it, a "fail" and a "success" are emotional concepts humans sort of invented. We are in love with them. We'd marry them if we could. We love them so much we want to be them. They're how we build identity.

It follows, then, that failing really sucks! It's hard to own it when it happens, and it can be wildly embarrassing. What's worse, our culture likes to highlight it. Examples are blooper reels, sports replays of a fall or foul, a starlet that tumbles on stage, or any other tabloid-ripe "bad" press, where critics drive home the shortcomings of a less-than-perfect effort made. We love winners *and* losers.

If we absolutely can't gawk at success or failure, any other extreme will do. Extremes are galvanizing and exciting and our culture is obsessed with them.

"Transformers! More than meets the eye."
–Transformers Theme Song

Good news for the non-extremists: superlatives aren't the only thing our culture is obsessed with! We also have a giant crush on transformation, as illustrated by every great storyline throughout history. Joseph Campbell wrote about it back in 1949 in *The Hero with a Thousand Faces*, describing the heroic cycle, with the pivotal point in every protagonist's journey being transformation. Change can't exist without the transformation.

Once most people get past the shock value of extremes, there is a need for substance and meaning. When a person or community meets change with transformation and growth, we just can't get enough of it.

Change is the domain of artists and creatives–observing pivot points, and ushering the world through the transitions with art, humor, books, films and design, etc.

Or in slightly more fancy-pants words:

"The way of the Creative works through change and transformation, so that each thing receives its true nature and destiny and comes into permanent accord with the Great Harmony: this is what furthers and what perseveres." –Alexander Pope

---

This project illuminated all kinds of surprise truths. One of them has to do with transformation: most failures (including my own) become the building blocks and tool kits for the successes that will come (and often can *only* come) at a later time.

Harkening back to maybe a page ago: It's like riding the Cyclone.

The fun and scary parts of the ride are all connected to the same rails–they are a part of the same experience, and though we would try to define one part as better or worse than the other, it is not so. Come to find out, one extreme literally fuels and turns into the other! The momentum of the plunge is 100% necessary to propel the roller coaster up the next incline! The fail is fodder for success.

But enough about you, let's talk about Meme

I have had some fun responses to the title of this book. One very talented musician even wrote to me and apologetically refused to interview because he did not want to be associated with anything related to failure. I said I respectfully understood. So far, most people love the title. I chose it because it really gets at the way our brains register our perception of good and bad.

If you have browsed any social network, or any news blog online in the last few years, you have definitely seen memes. The type of memes I'm referring to are viral ideas, not stemming from one source, but perpetuated by our collective grasp of a concept or truth. There aren't really rules to a meme, but its accuracy determines whether it will be "sticky" and, therefore passed along.

One popular meme (which I believe started as its own blog) is FAIL. This meme is a great example of how we obsess with extremes. Typically, this meme is presented as a snapshot or screenshot of something or someone seen in the world where, at a glance, it would be universally recognized as a total failure. Either as the caption or on the image, the only text is FAIL, with the exception of an occasional qualifier such as "parenting FAIL" or "pants FAIL". Shortly after this became popular, its opposite cropped up... with WIN or WINNING stamped on images of random observed victories.

Later, the qualifiers EPIC (for fail) and SUPER (for win) became common, too.

"There... are... four... lights." –Captain Picard

I've always loved the scene from Star Trek where Captain Picard is being held by enemy forces who are trying to break his will, in order to use him as an instrument for their purposes. One of the torture methods involved asking Picard repeatedly to count the four lights in front of him. The torturer insisted that there were five lights. Picard's will could not be broken.

Sometimes it is easy to acquiesce to the pull of cultural programming... those inside voices that tell you not to reach for success or risk failure because it's possible to find comfort by never leaving the space between. Those spaces will always be there as part of the spectrum.

When I took time to ponder where "my inside voices" really came from... I was mighty surprised at what I found. Now I have to be vigilant. Look deeper and trust my gut.

I'd say there are four things to note about navigating culture's love of failure:

One is that the label of failure is largely made up, therefore can be redefined.

I mean, if you're using the scientific method, sure... you could technically prove something failed or succeeded. However, the scientific method is based on supposing something–expecting something.

Take away the hypothesis... the element of expectation, and you just have neutral events. The experiment worked. The experiment did not work. What do you do? Another experiment. No tears. No need for a Scotch on the rocks or a phone call home to mum.

Our feelings about the results are subjective and emotional and comparative, and so often much bigger in our own minds than to the outside world. When the experiment is a test of our own capabilities, talents or prowess, we are naturally tough on ourselves and many of us relive the memory of our own personal mistakes over and over. Getting the perception of failure under control is the key to moving past it. Heck, that's why I am writing this, now!

The truth is that our most epic fails and super wins are both shades of the same learning process that makes up our lives. So, basically, it's within anyone's power to rewrite the emotional part of their own story, simply by connecting the dots from one part of the process to the next.

How rad is that?

The second thing is that we are likely rooting for one other.

Test it yourself! Watch a game, live performance or reality TV show. See the response when an athlete falls then gets back up and gets in the game, or a band keeps playing acoustic when the electricity cuts out. The crowd goes wild. That determination is electric and inspiring to audiences, and they'll either talk about the comeback or forget the mistake happened altogether. It's because of that transformation we love so much, and the chance to live vicariously in the rush of their roller coaster ride.

"There is no passion to be found playing small – in settling for a life that is less than the one you are capable of living." –Nelson Mandela

---

Success is a sort of strange experience, and it's outside of most people's comfort zones. For this reason, it's refreshing and inspiring when someone overcomes the thing that we all fear... when someone "goes there". It literally gives us permission to try for greatness, through example. It creates a pathway that is relatable and begs the question: "if s/he could do that, could I, as well?"

So, it's reassuring to know that at most people's core, they're rooting for the win, even if it's easy to be influenced by crowd-mentality. I think it's less common for individual people to genuinely "cheer on" failure.

The third thing is subtle. Self-deprecation and sarcasm can be toxic.

These two deadly killers make a social danger zone that must be traversed with great caution. Among the artists and creative people I know personally, there's a high percentage that *love them some sarcasm.* I am talking about dark, bitter, cutting sarcasm that infects groups of smart and talented people, then metastasizes into a bitter way of life. It's easy to get sucked in because the building blocks of this humor are usually observations based in fact or astute deductions about what's going on–the more "meta" the better. Not only am I guilty of gravitating toward friends, comedy and media that promote dark humor, but I'm a repeat offender, even when I know it contradicts my desire to be more optimistic.

Don't get me wrong. There is nothing wrong with this form of humor, and in my humble opinion, *any* use of humor is a great way to diffuse the tension of awkward and ugly realities. But, when a group or close friendship goes toxic, watch out! Slowly, the innocuous jokes and comments mutate into an addictive green goo... Maybe that's why they call it *jaded*–right?

An unchecked social through line of sarcasm and dismissive thinking sets an invisible trap for anyone with creative goals or dreams.

It happens like this: you (the creative person) have a group of friends that tend to see the pessimistic side of life. You and your friends often exchange witty banter highlighting the "lost cause" or "hopeless lameness" of something. It could be anything—work, your town, the government, career opportunities, other people around you. Your insights win you laughs and acceptance by the group.

When you (the creative person) want to go out and make your brilliant idea a reality, you consider what your friends will think. You naturally predict that they will have the same sarcastic and dismissive attitude toward your idea. If you've gone toxic, you decide not to do it.

"It's a trap!" –Admiral Ackbar (Return of the Jedi)

The trick is having a healthy "sarcasm immune system" so that your ideas don't become a reason to overstay your welcome on the failure side of the spectrum, for the sake of fitting in.

That leads me to the fourth consideration: motion trumps extremes.

We are always in motion until death. That means that as long as we keep working at something it's physically impossible to fail or succeed in a finite way, because the game is not yet over!

It kind of deflates the importance of the terms by default.

It also implies that we are able to begin anew, without limitation. There are no rules anywhere that suggest we can't reboot. It's just between you and the infinite, whether you consider yourself successful. That includes when, where and how.

So....

Success and failure are simple events that continuously follow and fuel one another until we stop or we die. Both events create excitement and tension which we love. Our emotions and social influences add gravity to either experience, causing us to transform and change for better or worse. Change requires motion, which keeps the cycle going. By managing our perception and expectations, we can be master roller coaster riders!

With that said, let's move on to the Introduction!

The story I'm about to tell was my personal catalyst for studying how creative people experience and respond to failure and success, and why people *keep going* after an *EPIC FAIL* to score a personal *super win*.

At first blush, it could appear as very personal story, or like a series of "first world problems," but I assure you, my intention with this book is not to create a forum for complaint or boasting, or to draw attention to my own reality check. It is to illustrate both rhythm and polarity through *real stories* of creative people's career extremes. I'm shining a light on the motion between the extremes, and how each person perceived what happened. I saw bits of myself in every story, and I think you will too!

Here's how I came to write the book...

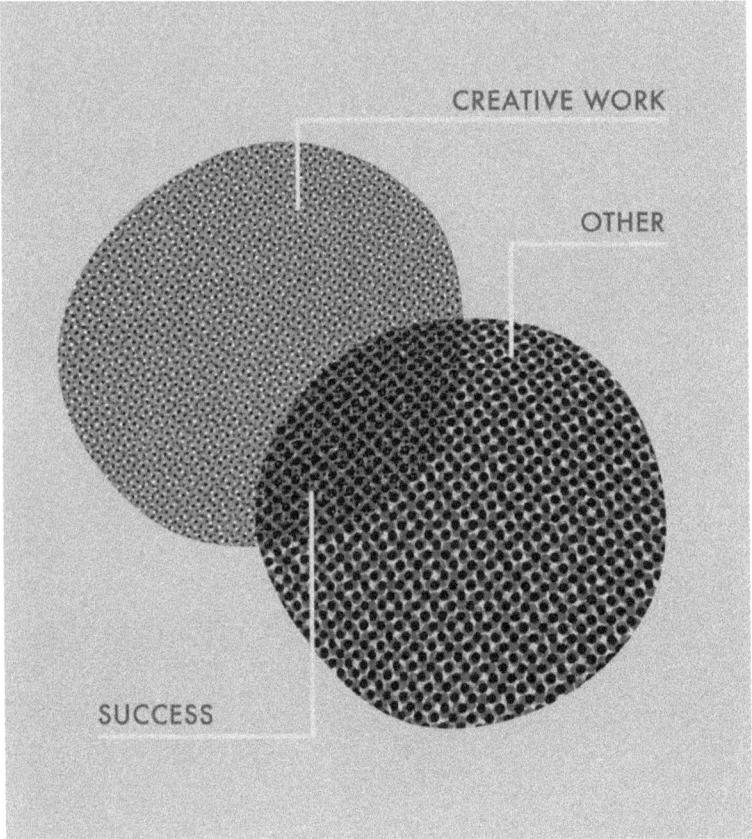

CREATIVE WORK

OTHER

SUCCESS

Introduction

Hijacked By Life & Punched In The Face By Friends

<BEGIN SPOILER ALERT>

Recently I re-watched Joss Whedon's Avengers, where all the characters come together through a risky plan devised by the enigmatic leader, Nick Fury. In the film, the villain, Loki, attempts to get inside of the minds of each superhero, turning them against one another. It's the old "divided we fall" trick.

At the beginning of the film, Loki quite literally gets into the minds of certain characters and under the grip of his superpowers, they lose their desire to think independently, and become his minions. One of the compromised characters is Clint Barton (Hawkeye), who is later saved by Natasha Romanoff (Black Widow) through a round of intense hand to hand combat.

Hawkeye: *"How'd you get him out?"*

Black Widow: *"Cognitive recalibration.*
...I hit you really hard on the head."

<END SPOILER ALERT>

This past winter, I was in what the kids call "a head space". I'll tell you what. I could have used some cognitive recalibration.

The holiday season was looming, and that meant my 35th birthday was around the corner too. Days were shortest in the year, and each day when I woke up, I shrank back under my covers in hopes that time would stop and the world would go away. It was the worst. It was like the winter blues on steroids.

On my birthday eve, I worked an overnight shift in retail, so I slept through most of my actual birthday. One girlfriend kindly invited me to breakfast, which somewhat redeemed the day, but the sinking feeling returned on my train ride home.

See, I had set this year as a milestone birthday for my creative career back in my early 20s. "By 35," I said, "I will be at my personal best. I'll have already succeeded in recording a great record, maybe have some hits, and I'll have built my reputation, and I'll be on to more sophisticated projects like being invited to compose for film, or collaborate with other successful artists." I thought I would surely be married by this age, and of course I'd have established myself.

However, the reality struck me that 35 looks nothing like what I imagined. I'm still single, I still freelance or hold a day job to pay rent, I'm releasing work but I'm certainly not signed to a major label, and I'm not necessarily being courted for fancy collaborations with famous people.

The following day, I tried to be cheerful. "By most standards, I have a great life, and I should be happy," I rationalized, "I've done a lot!" I brewed some coffee, and made a list of things to be thankful for, which didn't seem to help, but I did it anyway.

I still wanted to celebrate. I invited friends to come ice skating with me at a rink in the city, then come out for a drink followed by some ping-pong ball or air hockey. No one came. Not one person. I skated around the tiny oval rink solo in a mixed sea of kids and professional athletes for about 30 minutes, "Instagrammed" my skates for posterity, then loitered near the pizza concessions for another 15 minutes. Maybe someone would show up. One or two text messages came through–friends regretfully declining. Many apologies. Ugh.

I packed up my skates and made my way to the elevator which I shared with two precocious twin girls in purple sequined leotards. I did my best impression of a serious fun-haver as we were carried down to ground level. That's right. I was just out doing one of my favorite things that I loved sooo much that I'd do it alone on a Monday night. Once out of the athletic center, I rushed to the next activity on the itinerary, the bar at Ace Hotel.

Surely friends would join me for drinks. Drinks are easy!

Nope. I sat for a full hour and a half over a bourbon and a cheese plate with my phone on the counter. I started about ten text conversations with friends and family from away, so that it wouldn't appear that I was a loser to the chattering patrons on either side of me who were both couples. It became apparent that they were waiting patiently for me to relinquish my bar stool. That was the last straw. I heard nothing from the friends who hadn't declined by text, so I paid my tab, sent a message to my friends that ping-pong was canceled, and took the train back to Brooklyn, defeated.

This birthday was a failure. I started thinking about all the failures I'd ever had…and there are a lot…often intrinsically linked to something I'd successfully accomplished, or something others perceived as successful.

For example, I had, just months before, been nominated semi-finals as "Brooklyn Musical Artist of the Year" through a national arts organization. I was voted into the semi-finals by friends, family and fans. This involved a performance at the Brooklyn showcase. It was an immense honor and a thing to be proud of, right? The nomination was deeply touching, for sure. Somehow, though, remembering the showcase feels more akin to poking at a fresh bruise on my psyche. Why?

For the most part, the show was a success. I didn't win the title, but that had never been the point for me. The issue was my personal experience of that day.

All the memories of how it failed piled up in my mind... I relived it in vivid detail:

My assistant had canceled a couple of days before, and then my back-up assistant canceled at the last minute. I hauled all my equipment, merchandise & table dressings by myself on the subway, and then lugged it to the space to hit the strict check-in time, only to find I was there before any of the other bands, and wouldn't sound-check for hours. I was testing new equipment, to avoid a repeat of a total equipment failure I'd had the previous month. When I chatted with the sound guy, I discovered I was still missing certain cables I needed. I dashed off to Guitar Center, in the downtime. I got back after the other acts had finally arrived. We had a tight schedule. Despite my early arrival and attempts to be prepared, the other bands sound checked *several long songs*, leaving me only fifteen minutes to set up, sound check and break down. And... we couldn't get the equipment to work. Multiple people tried to assist, which further infuriated me because there were "too many cooks in the kitchen." The host of the event told me to wrap it up, and I hadn't made a noise! In the next five minutes, we managed to get sound, and do a workaround, then I was done. That's it. The performance would be "fly by the seat of my pants" at best.

I sank to my personal worst as far as attitude goes. I couldn't relax or enjoy myself. I managed to sing through my set, but I know the energy wasn't there. The spirit of what I was creating was crushed in the madness of the day, and the stress of doing it alone.

The showcase was well attended, but only one person came specifically to see me, then split. The judging depended on audience votes. Though many people had rallied for me to get there, I felt extremely isolated and alone at the event.

The worst thing is when that inner voice gets going because it not only relives things, it concludes things. And boy did my mind take me to that next step... *"You've lost your touch. It's been years since you've done a show like this... what are you doing? Be realistic? No one cares about a thirty-something musician rebooting her career... especially in Brooklyn. Maybe you are fooling yourself. You've never excelled at club shows... etc.. etc... etc...."*

Yes... this is how I spent my birthday; thinking about failure. Exhausting, right?

In the safety of my apartment, I wrapped myself in all of my blankets and called my friend Ken on the West Coast. We have been friends for nearly a decade and a half, and have always encouraged each other's creativity and artistic projects. Ken is a film editor. He is forever telling me I should be doing more with my creativity... that the world is full of opportunities I'm missing. It hurts because I work so hard at my art, but I know in some way he's right. I do a lot creatively–perhaps more than most, but I'm a "Jill of All Trades", and it's been tough to gain traction.

Ken listened as I recounted my tale of woe. I told him I was miserable, a failed musician and unhappy with how my life and my birthday were turning out. He asked me this question that rocked me to my core. He asked me what I really wanted to do to make a living. Not what I wanted for a side job... and not what I wanted for my personal art... but what did I ideally *want* to do every day to *make a living*.

OUCH. There it was.

The question I hate most... because it brings up an ugly social schism. *Creative types and traditional business do not mix. You can't make a living doing your art. Do it on the side, or do something similar to it. Never just the art. Not for a living. The odds of success are not in your favor.* Of course, Ken didn't imply this... he only asked what I wanted to do. I filled in all the blanks... or rather, years of cultural programming filled in the blanks.

Honestly, this wasn't what I'd been expecting when I called for a birthday chat, but it was precisely what I needed. It was a powerful catalyst, and it was exhausting. I got in bed and let my spinning mind sleep.

~

When I woke up, I began a relentless inventory of my actions, intentions, failures and successes–this time with a new purpose. I started thinking about archetypes; how did my story really compare with the creative community as a whole? The call with Ken had introduced a sub-question: What are the cultural messages artists and innovators are receiving and parroting back around success and career viability? I grew more and more curious about *the art of making a living as an artist.* Right now, my curiosity might even be eclipsing my other projects! It's a puzzle.

I like puzzles. The questions I was kicking around were eating at me.

How had it come to this? I know I'm not the only one who feels this way. Why is there a paradox-like pigeonhole to contend with, when we live in a vast world full of opportunities? Why do artists feel like they are destined to embody polarizing extreme poverty, closed off from financial success–*unless* they squeeze through the industry bottleneck and become a polarized extreme success. Is this dichotomy the same for all entrepreneurs, freelancers and innovators? We are obsessed with the highs and lows.

I found I was on fire to uncover the answers. I chewed on it some more. After a few weeks of feverish note-taking, research and introspection, I had another breakthrough. Something that felt like a move forward.

I thought, "What are my resources?" I dug out the list of thanks... In fact I went back and looked at all my lists of thanks (it's a journaling habit I've kept since my days at the University of Maine).

The common thread was people. *People!* Duh. I might as well have opened up that journal and found a million dollars hidden inside. I felt like Spiderman the second he realized he could swing from building to building.

Instantly the paradigm shifted.

I know people. Amazing people. People with stories.

I logged onto my social networking pages... cracked open the shoebox of business cards I'd been hoarding, and opened my address book. The immense amount of talent and history, trial and triumph, perseverance and faith was overwhelming.

That was it. I was going to write to some of the innovative people I know and ask for their candid stories around the existential questions I had been struggling with:

1. **What is failure, really?**
2. **What is success, honestly?**
3. **When you calculate the failure and the success, is a career worth it?**

For a brief moment, I cringed. Was I crowdsourcing therapy? Seriously? This is happening? Yes it is.

That is the moment I realized how unique it is, and how lucky I am to have such a network, and that is the moment I knew I'd write this book.

How helpful, I thought, could this be to other creatives out there, any age, any part of the world. These were the validating, and inspiring stories I needed in a dark moment; it's only fair to "pay it forward." I have a feeling this is one of those magnificent projects that will be worth every bit of work and sweat because it's much bigger than me.

I did not have the faintest idea how deeply I was going to get into this, but this book has certainly turned my thinking around... and it might just be the win on the the other side of my "epic" birthday fail.

Pandora's wardrobe

Another gem of a revelation cropped up from this little experiment. It became clear that I've unwittingly been solving this fail/success/living equation since I was in grade school. In doing so, I tried on about a dozen different career identities, like cheap dresses at H&M.

The more people I meet in the world, the more I can see that it's not uncommon in my generation to do this... we don't all have a clear and measurable path to success at this particular point in history because of the exponential change in our resources, communication tools and economy. It's a lot of trial and error.

I grew up in the quaint Bangor area, in the heart of Maine.

As a kid, I saw the opportunity to go into business for myself as a totally viable option. While my mother, father and step-mother taught me to embrace and love education, and I took to school naturally, many of the folks in my family had foregone college to make an independent trade-based living. My grandfather was an electrician, my uncle a painter and carpenter. Others fished. My mother worked in construction, and my father was a chef. My step-mom was a kindergarten teacher.

In school, I was quite the little artist... and I was forever making workarounds and negotiating with teachers and advisors to do projects instead of papers, or whatever non-traditional format was available. Just like every other kid, I was told that marvelous story at an early age... you know the one. It goes like this:

"You can be anything you want to be when you grow up."

I wanted to be *a lot* of things–a painter, a singer-songwriter, a U.N translator, an art therapist, a book author, a filmmaker, a poet.

I actually believed that story 100%. Other than the U.N. Translator, I have literally tried out all these things! But trust me, it hasn't been pretty.

The qualified twist

There is a problem with the story. It's missing all the freaking qualifiers!

Just. Can you be just one thing? How specific does it have to be? Can you combine dreams and be a ballerina-author, or a musician-painter?

You will get a mixed response if you ask this question! Some people say you have to focus, and other people say you can leverage each thing to enrich your career.

Successful. Can you be a "successful" ballerina, "well-paid" poet, "best-selling" author, "famous musician"? If so, how is it done?

Then there is the question of measurable standards. Successful according to who? Well-paid in relation to what? Best-selling in what industry? Famous in what niche?

Are we relegated to measuring success through financial gain? It can seem that way, when you ask around, right?

If so, how boring!

When I was a little girl it was the 80s, and back then things were a little more polarized... also media was not what it is today. There was no Internet.

There was also very little teaching around the differences between deciding who you want to be, and deciding what you want to do for a living. I mean, society pretty well merges these things in some fields. In my graduating class, those wanting to be doctors, lawyers, scientists, teachers could expect a neatly defined roadmap to a canonized idea of success in their fields. Little did we all know that the giant many-armed ecommerce and technology monster would come and make our world magnificently messy.

In a way it's leveling the playing field. It's also scary. Like a natural disaster, that gives everyone a clean slate, and a lifetime of work. But, I digress.

If I could go back in time, I would have listed inventor as a career aspiration, because that is what I really am. Because there was no class on creating income from your passion, and configuring your inner success-ometer, I spent some 20 years inventing my personal skills and tools from scratch. It has to be done.

Turns out, we're all inventors.

Call it an early mid-life crisis, call it madness... call it just what the doctor ordered. My birthday melt-down led me to crash hard into the quandaries that have haunted creative types for centuries. I felt like Gandalf fighting the Balrog. I had to let go of some links to past thinking in order to take on a new challenge. I feel I've come out the other side very much myself, but with a new set of eyes.

There are hard questions that need answering, astonishing possibilities that need seizing. Without a doubt, our world has become more individual, more challenging, more demanding, more connected, faster, meaner, and exponentially more competitive. Good news is: the answers to the questions are everywhere!

Even traditional careers industries are being rethought, downsized, mobilized, and reformed. I believe the time to be a creative is exactly this moment.

At the rate things are changing, re-imagining the very roots and trappings of success will become a basic skill set. The inventive and the adaptable will be able to define things, starting from wherever they are, while the "ladder to success" will be abandoned in favor of more flexible and creative possibilities.

It's already happening.

First we'll have to look at our thinking. Then, it's time to get our creativity on.

We're individuals, but not alone.

What follows is a collection of interviews with 27 creative, self-made people, replete with challenges, triumphs, failures and successes. I asked each person to draw a connection between their personal bests and worsts, and to share what inspires them to stay in the game.

I reached out to friends I know in music, filmmaking, tech, freelance art & design, performing arts, and small business. There are so many fields and wonderful people that could be added, but this is where I could personally begin.

A final note

These are *regular* people like you and me, telling real stories and revealing very personal fears and realities about their careers. Most all come from humble beginnings, and many of them balance between their passion and a day job, or did for years before making the passion into a full-time career. Every one of them has built their personal successes through gusto, hard work and creative thinking.

I think you'll be charmed and moved by just how relatable the stories are, and I hope to keep the dialogue going on my blog and networking sites.

Best,

Serena

Michele Wehrwein Albion

AUTHOR, MOM

"In retrospect, those rejection letters were the best thing that ever could have happened to me."

We were at a very sad gathering. It was the funeral of my beautiful cousin, who died of Huntington's. There were a lot of people there. Apparently, many of us are related.

After my stepmom's passing a year earlier, I got to know my dad's side of the family better at the celebration of life. It had been years since we'd all gathered in one place. This was another such occasion. Sad, and yet we bonded there.

I met Michele at the reception. She was witty and aware, and used top notch vocabulary. I was very happy to chat with her and find out more about our relationship. Turns out she has written a book or two, and is extremely cool.

Michele is holding down a brave combo: being a mom and traveling as an author. How she does it? I will never know!

To me, what stands in her story is that she made a bold career shift. I see her updates about library touring and the ways she is sharing her work. It's an inspiration, and it gives me courage to go out and try my hand at something unknown!

~

What was your first job ever?

From the time I made the stunning realization that Little House on the Prairie came before The Waltons historically--I was about six--I have been a history nerd.

Naturally, my first job at the age of fifteen was working at a Fort Western Museum. I tromped around the 1754 fort in period costume; which looked cute on the other guides, but on me bore a hopelessly unflattering likeness to the St. Pauli Girl. Still, I loved the job. I felt a personal victory when one of my visitors made a historical connection. I'm very grateful for that first experience. Later I worked backstage at the Maine State Museum.

Talk about how you felt after high school versus today on the question "what do you want to be when you grow up?"

Graduating from high school was terrifying for me. I was one of those kids who didn't have much of a safety net. I knew whatever I did, I had to do it well because there was no going home again.

I was very goal oriented and decided to be a museum curator before I entered college. Before orientation I had researched the academic requirements, laid out my courses for four years and argued with my counselor about the efficacy of these plans. I worked hard, got good grades and did eventually become a curator.

I did succeed in becoming what I wanted to be "when I grew up," but the downside was that I was so afraid to fail that I didn't take the risks and enjoy high school or college the way I should have. We learn things by making mistakes--socially as well as academically--and I made plenty of those, but I feel like I would have benefitted from taking more risks.

In recent years, I've tried to push myself to redefine what I want to be "when I grow up," and take more risks and put myself out there professionally. Being a mother with four children under 16, the risks are small, but as I tell my kids, the only people who don't make mistakes are the ones who don't actually do anything.

What do you do today to make a living?

Ha! Make a living? I'm not sure I'm actually making a living, but I'm working on it.

I'm the author of four books: The Florida Life of Thomas Edison, The Quotable Edison, The Quotable Henry Ford, and The Quotable Eleanor Roosevelt.

I have two fiction works in process and I'm gearing up to take the risk of starting to send them out to agents and publishers.

Describe the worst moment of failure in your creative/ entrepreneurial career.

My senior year of college I figured I had my career path all sewn up. I had stellar grades, had been working in museums for years, graduated Phi Beta Kappa and had glowing references from my professors. I applied to three different graduate schools so I could earn my Masters and become a curator. No problem.

The site visits and interviews went along swimmingly and I waited for those acceptance envelopes to slide into my dorm room mailbox. They did. Two rejections, one right after the other. I was devastated. I did everything right, didn't I? I had assumed I would get into graduate school and had no backup plans for a job. I had no place to live, no place to go.

Weeks later the third envelope came. Thankfully it was an acceptance letter. I was so relieved. My life wasn't over.

In retrospect, those rejection letters were the best thing that ever could have happened to me. Both the programs I didn't get into were very small and geographically isolated.

The George Washington University museum studies program was located in Washington DC. While getting my Masters, I had a wide variety of opportunities, including working at The US Holocaust Memorial Museum, which hadn't yet opened. Also, growing up in rural Maine, I had been afraid of living in a big city. I found I loved it. I never had to be afraid of urban living again.

Describe the best success you've experienced in your field.

After graduate school I landed my first full-time museum job. At the age of 25 I achieved my lifetime goal of becoming curator at The Edison & Ford Winter Estates in Fort Myers, Florida. It was a hollow victory.

The words "now what?" surged through my brain. It was time for a new goal.

I had always loved to write, but never considered it a career choice. My entire childhood, I never met a writer. Being one was as unobtainable as becoming the Queen of England. But shortly after being hired, I took a risk. I contacted the Fort Myers newspaper and asked them if they'd be interested in a monthly column on Thomas Edison's life in Florida. They said yes.

The first columns were awful, but eventually I got my feet under me. I found both the research and the writing thrilling. After a few years I decided I wanted to write a book about Edison's life in Florida. It took me ten years of research and writing (and I had four children during that time too), but eventually the manuscript was complete. It took all the gumption I had to send it out to a publisher. One publisher. I was fully expecting a thin rejection letter to arrive in my mailbox. So when I received the phone call, I was so astounded I couldn't speak. The editor actually called me to say they wanted the manuscript. I was over the moon.

Researching, writing, rewriting and finding the time to write with my crazy life is challenging, but it provides such a high when someone says, "Hey, I enjoyed your book."

Is there a connection to you between them?

No one likes to fail, but I haven't been able to succeed without falling on my face here and there. Now, with a few years under my belt, I am trying hard to embrace it. You can't succeed at something unless you're willing to take a risk. Not all risks are going to result in success. But the alternative is stagnation. I just can't live with stagnation.

Did you ever think of quitting or giving up, and more importantly why did you keep going?

Giving up is not in my nature, but I've been close a few times over the years.

When hit in the face with a significant failure I crawl up in a metaphorical fetal position for a while and allow myself a pity party. I suppose it's a grieving process, mourning for the lost opportunity. But no one wants to be at that party long, least of all me. I put it behind me and try to move on. Sometimes the process is quick and sometimes it's a long lingering ache. Either way, it's important for me to acknowledge my responsibility in the failure. Without that, I'm not going to be able to move on. I'll just keep making the same mistakes over and over.

In this crazy world, what is your best advice for a budding entrepreneur, artist, or innovator?

Failure is a bitch. It shakes you to your core. It shoves you face down in the dirt. But people who make real successes of themselves, professionally and personally are willing to take that risk. You can't succeed unless you're willing to fail.

Mary Bee

SINGER & MARKETING DIRECTOR

> "...Even if it ruins my street cred for life - I watched the Britney Spears movie, and it made me decide to follow my passion."

A bit ago Mary was tending bar at AS220, and I was there on a slow evening with some friends. I thought she was the sunshiniest person I'd ever seen in that place. At the time I had been surrounding myself with a lot of angsty artists.

I found out that I knew her brother Will. He is a magician and musician. I asked her what she did, and she said that she was a singer. It wasn't until much later that I heard her sing; literally years later. So beautiful.

We were never close, but she was another who made the big move out to the West Coast. What's more, she found her way into a well-suited job with a very helpful organization that supports the music industry. I was so impressed by this.

I briefly got to see Mary when I last visited California. I actually attended one of the events she helped coordinate, and as I was putting this book together, she came to mind right away.

Sometimes a little sunshine (and hard work) goes a long way!

~

What was your first job ever?

My Father's business, 'Palmer River Canoe'/'Canoe Passage Outfitters'.

Talk about how you felt when you graduated high school versus how you feel now about the question "what do you want to be when you grow up?"

It's very strange how much I am doing what I wanted to do when I grew up. I always want to do more and I have a long ways to go of course, but I feel incredibly blessed where I am right now.

What do you do today to make a living?

Singing and working at NARIP (National Association of Record Industry Professionals).

Describe the worst moment of failure in your creative/ entrepreneurial career.

The first time I sang at the Santa Monica Promenade, I was by myself and in the middle of my first song and somehow lost my balance. I fell backwards tripping over a low fence into a bunch of flowers and wood chips surrounding a giant hedge sculpture dinosaur.

Describe the best success you've experienced in your field.

So far my most exciting success was playing myself and singing in a cartoon 'Explosion Bus' created by and starring one of my favorite comedians, Johnathan Katz (Dr. Katz, Professional Therapist). It was probably one of the funnest experiences I've had, and being in cartoons has always been a dream for me.

What's the connection?

They were both a risk. Sometimes you fall (literally), but everything takes you to the next step.

> "Learn the business of what you are entering into
> so that you are informed and do not have to
> rely on others to make big decisions for you."

Did you ever think of quitting or giving up, and more importantly why did you keep going?

There was one short period of my life when I was about 20, I thought I would get a 'normal' job in the medical field or something like that because music might be too hard (I actually worked at a psych hospital that year). I will be 100% honest with you, even if it ruins my street cred for life - I watched the Britney Spears movie, and it made me decide to follow my passion - HA!

In this crazy world, what is your best advice for a budding entrepreneur, artist, or innovator?

Work HARD. Make a great product. Spend time creating something quality to promote and sell. Learn the business of what you are entering into so that you are informed and do not have to rely on others to make big decisions for you. Be good to people along the way and it will come back to you. :)

.

Eno Freedman Brodmann

FILMMAKER, DJ

"I'd like to think the best way to fix a mistake is to bury it under many more improvements."

"Nice pants," I said. "Oh thanks," said Eno. "Hey, stand in front of me and wrap your arms around me backwards, then just start talking," I instructed. "Um. Okaay," he said, following the instructions..." Eno and I had worn the same ridiculous shade of mustard to work...His pants, my shirt. I proceeded to gesticulate with my arms as he talked about random things. It's an old improv theater exercise. I think there still may be a video of this lurking on someone's phone... If so, please get in touch with me!

Later on, I found out that Eno was 1) impossibly young for his level of social maturity. 2) an amazing DJ and musician, as well as videographer. 3) really sweet and held in high regard by other creative friends of mine.

He played the launch event for the fundraising campaign that helped me release this book and bring it out on the road.

What I noticed about Eno is that he is a super-champ at networking, and it never feels like networking. He is low-key and able to get along with just about anyone. It doesn't look like work. I think I'll always be in awe of that.

~

What was your first job ever?

I had taken a year off after high school and decided to travel and study abroad. I had become so close to my friends and group that I feared a long summer break before college would be empty and lonely.

I decided to apply to some jobs around New York where I live and ended up with an interview at an Apple Store near Columbus Circle. Coincidentally, that is where I met Serena and many other talented people. I became a specialist and sold pads and pods to foreigners and a few locals. With school taking off, it began to prove a challenge and I started working early morning shifts before school. I had grown exhausted and left the position after a year and a half. I was twenty years old.

Talk about how you felt after high school versus today on the question "what do you want to be when you grow up?"

Since ten I had wanted to become a filmmaker and musician so I always had a pretty clear direction of the field I wanted to work in. At graduation I knew I was going to NYU for Film Production and was pretty serene. I remember a very anti-climactic graduation. Many people cried and celebrated but it felt natural. I was ready to leave high school and start my year off. I was eager.

What do you do today to make a living?

Right now, I'm still finishing up a degree for film production at NYU. I do sound mixing and film scoring for friends and clients when I can, to make a little extra.

Describe the worst moment of failure in your creative/ entrepreneurial career.

I had worked months promoting a show I was doing sound and music for. It was a rainy Sunday in Brooklyn, and I had put together a bill of acts who proved they could bring people. Through a music connection, I had even secured support from a Grammy Nominated producer of Groove Collective. We had many people planning to attend and I had promised the hall a certain draw. I had never played a venue as big. By the end of the night, we had successfully brought six people to the show (four of whom were on the guest list). With drinks aside I don't think the venue made more than $20 that night. I was ashamed but thought I could take some energy out on stage performing. Our cables failed and we lost sound to a huge amount of feedback. After ten minutes of broken technology, I walked off stage. No performance was even held. I'm sure I was blacklisted to book there again.

Describe the best success you've experienced in your field.

On my study abroad we decided to film an original music video with original music about American youth in Jerusalem. Our video became very popular on YouTube, at points earning 1K hits daily. We decided to post on the video that we were going to play some songs from the film live at a bar in the city. The place was packed wall to wall. We had a five minute performance and we had people we had never seen with signs supporting the music video and dancing everywhere. It was a great feeling.

Is there a connection?

Perhaps. I feel embarrassed about the night at that club but no one remembers it in the long run. I ended up playing a big show there a few months ago for Sandy relief and had a blast. The circle has met its end. I'd like to think the best way to fix a mistake is to bury it under many more improvements. I'm sure there will be films I screen of mine where no one laughs, or no one comes to fill in the seats. It's a process. The night of random fame in the Jerusalem bar was also inspiring. At the time I remember there was a lot of drama with kids on the program, and being all out together dancing brought the group together. We were all so proud of each other.

Did you ever think of quitting or giving up, and more importantly why did you keep going?

I've had times where I focused more on one discipline than the other. There have also been moments where I didn't feel inspired to make music or art. Then I just get sad about my loss of passion and make art to get me to cope. It's a wonderfully backward cycle.

In this crazy world, what is your best advice for a budding entrepreneur, artist, or innovator?

A few pieces of advice. First, one who makes no mistakes, makes nothing at all. Second, listen to those around you and learn from everyone. If you are a sponge taking everyone's advice and information, you will gain more than caring about your ego and protecting it. Last, learn how to take criticism like its your job. Incorporate change advised by others and grow with your team. Collaborate.

Dennis Carroll

CEO OF A MEDIA PRODUCTION COMPANY

"Great thing about working for someone else is
the normalcy of it. Paychecks every other Friday,
health insurance, a regular schedule.
But I wasn't doing what I loved."

To me, Dennis will always be "Zippy".

I was one of the people grand opening a new big box music
equipment store in North Attleboro, Mass. The place was being
built from the ground up, from the paint on the walls to scanning
and sku-ing all the new merchandise and getting it out on the floor.
Every department had to get people trained up and oriented, while
the place was literally being built around us.

I was sort of assigned by default to lead the pro-audio and keyboard department, since most everyone else onboard had a background in guitar gear. Back then I was a plain old piano player. I
knew not a thing about keyboards (or electronics for that matter). I
learned it all, but not without the help of a few rockin' vets,
brought in to help launch things. Zippy was one of them.

I said to the store manager... "I'm going to get trained by a guy
named Zippy?" I later found out why he was called that. I had
never met someone with so much energy in my entire life. He was
happy and fun, and knew more about MIDI, keyboards and building complex digital audio setups than anyone I had ever met.

This is a bit of a recurring theme, but once again, I found myself
making ends meet in a corporate retail environment. Zippy was
that person who stands out as real in a wash of corporate and sta-
tus quo nonsense. Despite the intensity and sales structure that we
all had to funnel ourselves through, he brought his personality to

every single action and conversation. This is paramount to survival. It was a sign that it was possible. I did my best to emulate that in whatever I did.

Thirteen years later, I checked in to see what he was up to online. Awesome! He took his expertise and got entrepreneurial with it. I love to hear that, and I'm immensely proud to share this interview with you.

~

What was your first job ever?

I was a busboy at a restaurant my grandfather managed. I worked all summer so I could save up enough money to buy a drum set.

The minute I had saved enough money I quit.

Talk about how you felt after high school versus today on the question "what do you want to be when you grow up?"

I have a different view of my high school years now 20 years later than what apparently really happened. I remember high school and not having a ton of friends but knowing a lot of people. I remember being a pretty quiet, introverted individual. Facebook being the great "gatherer of people you used to know" has put me in touch with most of the people I would want to be in touch with from my high school. Reconnecting with some of my class and talking about the "good 'ole days" has changed my perspective of my high school days. I knew a lot of people who had put themselves under the pressure of "what am I going to do now?" like the end of high school signified the beginning of the end of allowable fuckups. Up until then it was ok to screw up as much as you wanted to but now every single decision from here on out was going to be important and change my life for the better or for the worse. But that wasn't me. I never once felt the stress of "what am I going to be when I grow up?" because I loved music, I loved movies, I knew they were going to play a part in my career path because isn't that what we all end up doing? Doing what we love? The trick was figuring out how I was going to incorporate these passions in to a career.

What do you do today to make a living?

I am a freelance media producer. On the audio side I produce and engineer records for musicians. I also compose and write original music for film and television. On the video side I do everything from shooting to post production, editing and animating. Corporate video, commercials, trade show video, really a bit of everything.

Describe the worst moment of failure in your creative/ entrepreneurial career.

My biggest misstep was in 2007. I was working on my biggest project to date and quite possibly still my biggest project even today. I was hired by comedian Robert Kelly and Comedy Central to shoot behind the scenes footage of the making of Bobby's new comedy CD. Bobby had just finished an HBO series with Dane Cook called Tourgasm.

For both of us it was our first big career test. Bob had attracted the attention of Comedy Central and I was on board to shoot something that potentially was going to be seen by hundreds of thousands of people. I shot 70 hours of footage for a 45 minute documentary. We traveled all over the country, LA, Vegas, NYC, and Boston. Bobby had arranged for some really talented people to be in this thing. Dane Cook, Colin Quinn, Jim Norton, the list goes on. And I feel that if I had exited the project having just shot it, turning it over to Comedy Central to edit, everything would have been great.

However, when we were wrapping up principle shooting in Boston I met with Bobby and threw my name in the hat to stay on and direct and edit the film. Up to this point he had loved what we had done together so it didn't take much convincing. Comedy Central gave it the OK and we were off and running. The problem was that I wasn't ready for this kind of responsibility.

Personally, I was in a bad place in my life. I had recently gone through a divorce, I was full of self-doubt, and I really had no direction in my life. Outside of my work I was wreck and for the first time all the personal demons were affecting my career. And it showed in the final product. This was my big moment, a chance to break through and I failed. Hard. And worse, I let a lot of people down.

I'm in a much better place now but I do look back on that one project and I regret not being able to give it everything. And regret sucks.

Describe the best success you've experienced in your field.

There have been a lot of little successes.

I had the fortune of working with Aerosmith for 4 years. Got my name in the thank yous of a couple records and had Joe Perry play some guitar on a song I wrote.

I've had the privilege to work with so many talented artists from musicians to illustrators and painters who have inspired me in different ways.

But I think for me, the biggest success, though not directly related to my work, was marrying my wife Erica last summer. For me, a solid, happy personal life keeps me focused and motivated. Having her love and support has really made me want to be better at what I do.

How do you connect the two?

I overanalyze everything. I try to learn from every experience. Take away the positives and learn from the negatives. What worked with that project and what didn't work with that project? I try to draw parallels along different experiences to find common positives.

Did you ever think of quitting or giving up, and more importantly why did you keep going?

Ha. I did. In October of 2010 I took a job in music retail. In January 2011 I sold off the assets of my company. I was playing it safe.

Great thing about working for someone else is the normalcy of it. Paychecks every other Friday, health insurance, a regular schedule. But I wasn't doing what I loved. I was taking the occasional project here and there but my schedule didn't really allow much.

In September 2012 I got a phone call from the marketing head of a big tax preparation company who I had worked with when she was at Hartz years before. She asked if I was still doing media production. Her company wanted a fresh take on some of the promotional videos they were producing. I said sure. It ended up being a national campaign and they gave me 100% creative license. The campaign was a big success and I found myself quoting Al Pacino from The Godfather (Part 3). "Just when I thought I was out, they pull me back in."

I'm back at it. Doing 14-20 hour days, 6 days a week. Most of it sitting in front of a Mac, chopping and animating. And I absolutely love it.

In this crazy world, what is your best advice for a budding entrepreneur, artist, or innovator?

Stay focused on your goals. It's easy to get distracted.

Don't give up. I got a fortune cookie once that read "A person can fail many times but you are not a failure until you give up."

Surround yourself with good people. People who love you. Family, friends. Weed out the negatives in your life. They are there only to side track you from your goals.

That hour you spent watching a rerun of CSI Miami could have been better spent networking online, being creative, or learning a new aspect of your business.

There are a lot of people out there who are doing what you do. How are you going to do it better or different?

Be social.

Gavin Castleton

MUSICIAN, UX DESIGNER, INNOVATOR

"I think it's unhealthy to believe in big breaks."

I first met Gavin playing a show with his band at the Met in Providence, RI. He was a monster on stage, and my friend Ron mentioned him by name. This was way back in 1999, I believe.

As with most Providence folks, we ran into each other on "the scene" for years. He was always loosely part of something I was loosely part of. Later he branched out as a solo artist, and his work was really compelling to me.

Sadly, I missed Gavin's NYC show a couple of years ago, and I had wanted to go badly. At the time, I had just been reminded of him through a crazy path of research I was doing on web design. I spotted his name in the credits of the site for a company that builds synthesizer sample banks for Ableton. Go figure!

However oddly connected, I reached out to Gavin for an interview, and am very excited to share it with you!

~

What was your first job ever?

I had a paper route when I was 14 or so.

Talk about how you felt after high school versus today on the question "what do you want to be when you grow up?"

I've had the same ambition since I was very little: "I want to make stuff." Around the time I graduated high school I was convinced that music should be my first priority.

What do you do today to make a living?

Music, UX design, and freelance web design.

Describe the worst moment of failure in your creative/ entrepreneurial career.

I performed live on KCRW in 2009 or so and I really blew it. I was in the throes of a lung infection, I was not disciplined enough in regards to my vocal exercising, my equipment was not dependable, and my band was a bit under-rehearsed. It was a huge opportunity for me and I did not execute very well. In the middle of our first and most important song of the set, my midi controller triggered a drum sample from an entirely different song. At that point my nerves gave out and I could barely sing anything after that. I just wanted to quit everything at that point.

Describe the best success you've experienced in your field.

This is hard for me to answer. My career doesn't really consist of peaks like that. It's been more of a series of tiny steps that comprise a very, very gradual incline (sometimes it's so gradual that it feels flat). I have had wonderful opportunities to open for big national acts. I've had my music featured on this show or that blog... but none of that is really the "big break" you'd think it would be.

I think it's unhealthy to believe in big breaks.

I think I felt more successful talking to young musicians who site my work as inspirational to their own than I did performing on Jimmy Fallon last year. I think just finishing a self-booked tour without losing money felt more successful than opening up for Taking Back Sunday for a block of shows.

How do you connect the two?

Any experience is an opportunity for growth. I try to have the objectivity to see them that way. Both the best and worst moments I mentioned were about work. My best moments came from hard work, my worst moments were due to a lack of hard work (or at least smart work) - so there's a connection.

Did you ever think of quitting or giving up, and more importantly why did you keep going?

I only think of quitting or giving up. Doing what you love can be the hardest thing in the world to do. I only keep going because there's still more in me to get out. When I'm empty, I'll stop.

In this crazy world, what is your best advice for a budding entrepreneur, artist, or innovator?

My advice for the entrepreneur would be: be prepared to start over, constantly.

My advice for the artist would be: As much as you may want to avoid the business side of your artistic endeavors, doing so will most likely mean you have a very short career as an artist. If you want the time to develop your craft into expertise, you've got to get a firm grip on your business model.

My advice for the innovator would be: look at the field you're trying to get into. Is it over-saturated? Is there enough room and public support to actually innovate or will you be dedicating your life to subtle variations of someone else's work? Why just adopt a pre-established medium when you could invent a new one?

Stella Chuu

COSPLAY & BURLESQUE ARTIST

"No one gets away with doing anything half-assed."

"What are those?" I said.

"Pasties!" she replied with a grin.

"Oh!" I said.

It was during Hurricane Irene and I was holed up in Astoria taking shelter. My neighborhood in Gowanus was right on the flood line. There were about eight of us staying in the house, and while we had a bit of cabin fever, spirits were high.

Stella was sewing sequins onto her creations and providing color commentary while the rest of the group was watching old TV episodes and playing video games. She has an infectious laugh and playful nature. It was nice to be around someone like that in a crisis situation. She even made cookies!

Later, I discovered that she is a talented graphic designer and burlesque dancer, who creates her own elaborate cosplay pieces and stage-wear. I went with a group of friends to see her perform, and she really delivers a full story onstage. I saw her perform in a Tron costume. For a moment I forgot that I was in an audience in a small theater, and just allowed myself to get lost in the swirl of glow-in-the-dark markings on the costume, and the circles of light in each of her hands. It was mesmerizing.

I think she is a great example of just owning your own style and creativity, and fearlessly sharing it with people despite the potential for criticism. Because she enjoys what she does, it's easy to embrace and encourage her creativity. Her art lets people acknowledge the child-like indulgence we all sort of crave, but perhaps hold back on.

What was your first job ever?

My first [career] gig was D20 Burlesque. I kittened for their 8bit Beauties Burlesque show and also debuted at their Internet Memes Burlesque Show.

What do you do today to make a living?

I perform about 3-4 nights per week. All the money I make off burlesque goes to funding my cosplays. I don't make any money off cosplaying.

Describe the worst moment of failure in your creative/ entrepreneurial career.

I've had a few failed gigs. Either my music wouldn't play, I forgot a costume item, or the show was just produced terribly. Its difficult to go home at the end of the night as the sun is rising and realizing you only made a few dollars for 4 hours of work.

Describe the best success you've experienced in your field.

My internet notoriety is my best bragging right. I have 21,000 fans on Facebook. It means that 21,000 people thought I was cool enough to follow.

Do you draw any connections between flopped gigs and social media success?

I keep the mantra that I am just one human being. I know that I've created a public image for myself and am quickly gaining fame. But my focus is my art. I am my own worst critic and I'll keep producing work that fulfills my needs.

Did you ever think of quitting or giving up, and more importantly why did you keep going?

I've wanted to give up cosplay a few times. It is an incredibly expensive hobby with absolutely no monetary reward. But the worst part is that the community is a mean girls club. No matter what you do, someone hates you and will try to ruin your fun. We are all narcissistic elitist peacocks.

In this crazy world, what is your best advice for a budding entrepreneur, artist, or innovator?

Only passionate people will succeed.

No one gets away with doing anything half-assed.

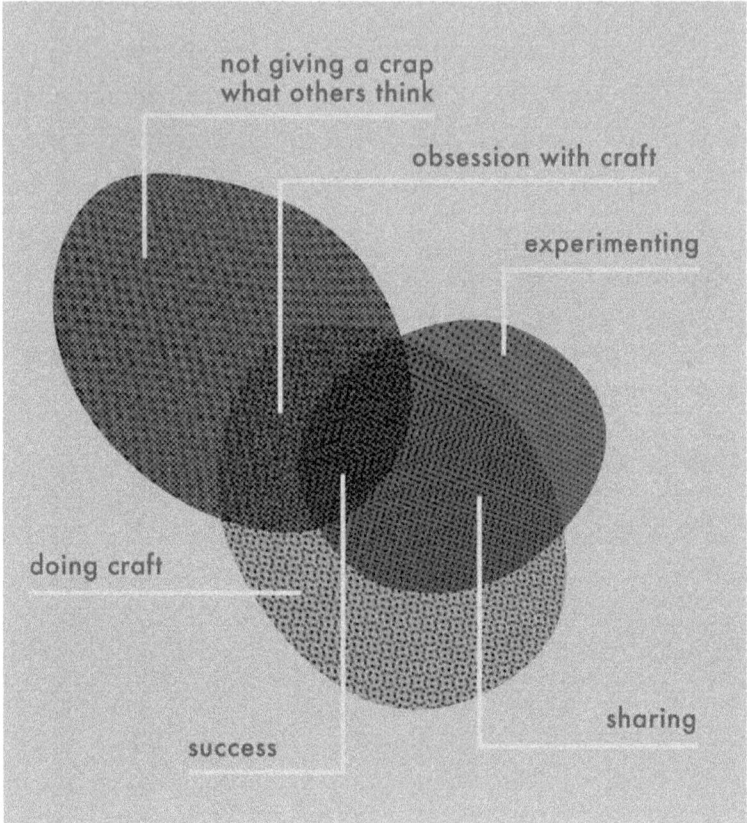

not giving a crap
what others think

obsession with craft

experimenting

doing craft

success

sharing

Jon Costantini

FILM DIRECTOR, TECH SUPPORT SUPERVISOR

"I think if I could go back, I would tell my young self to grow a thicker skin and become more comfortable with failure."

I met Jon the day I helped my friend Jaycen move into his apartment. They had been longtime friends, and I could immediately see why. They share a very similar sense of humor, and bicker like an old married couple.

Most of the day was spent just carrying boxes, but toward the end, Jon needed to bring back the moving truck. I was designated navigator, and Jaycen stayed behind.

It could have been awkward, but we just launched into a very interesting conversation about film, the music industry, careers, and the various and sundry implications of being "our age". The chat extended over Dunkin' Donuts, and I think it's fair to say that's when we became friends.

Film can be an extremely expensive and time consuming medium. I thought of Jon for the book because of how he strikes a balance in chasing his passion. My hope was to recreate a little of the conversation we had on moving day.

I hope you enjoy!

~

What was your first job ever?

I was a Bus Boy and ran the Sunday Brunch Buffet at a local high end restaurant part-time while I was in my Freshman year of high school. I remember fondly being molested by some of the waitresses, eating nearly as much food as I served, and spending way too much time washing dishes when it technically wasn't my job. It was my first taste of being a part of a large, decidedly dysfunctional work family. It was also my first experience with a temperamental boss. I vividly remember him frisbee-ing a large serving tray across the main dining room at a waitress - and hitting a customer.

Talk about how you felt after high school versus today on the question "what do you want to be when you grow up?"

The answer hasn't changed a bit. Filmmaker. My plan to get there... Well, I've come to realize that no one is going to just give you an opportunity. You need to earn it, make it yourself, or put yourself in the best position to cross paths with one. Admittedly, I'm still sort of a child at heart and don't want to lose the sense of discovery or naiveté that comes with that. However I have come to the realization that in order to create what you want at a high level, you need to take calculated risks and be able to back up your vision with a competent path to execute it.

What do you do today to make a living?

I'm a technical support supervisor in a flagship retail electronics store in New York City.

Describe the worst moment of failure in your creative/ entrepreneurial career.

Making the submission deadline to enter a short into

Sundance, which was a down-to-the-wire accomplishment - and then not even making it through the first round of submissions. I worked extremely hard on that project for about a year, invested some of my own money, the vast majority of my free time, called in every favor, etc. - and the dream was casually dashed in a few weeks.

Describe the best success you've experienced in your field.

The best success I've had has been more personal - someone sincerely telling me they enjoyed my work or picked out a specific detail that they connected with. I did some video content for a work meeting once, and one of the bosses said he knew it was my work the second it started. He said he recognized my style. A jump scare at the end of a short I directed actually making viewers jump.

Is there a connection? If so, what is it? Explain.

I think if I could go back, I would tell my young self to grow a thicker skin and become more comfortable with failure. I've come to learn that failure may be the most important aspect of ultimately becoming successful. Almost prerequisite. The failures always force me to look inward and be brutally honest with myself. Usually I end up finding out where I compromised, where I didn't use my ingenuity to solve a particular issue or where I wasn't being realistic with myself. The sincere praise, which doesn't necessarily come often, or unsolicited, is what really keeps me going through those hard times. To know that even fleeting moments of my vision connected with someone motivates me to fight harder for my voice to shine through on the next project. Most of what I do is about communication, and finding more and more effective ways to communicate is the name of the game.

Did you ever think of quitting or giving up, and more importantly why did you keep going?

Of course. We all have doubts. But as cliché as it is, this is my dream since I was a little kid. There are people in I've known all of my life that had similar aspirations when they were young. I've seen many of them give up their dreams to the responsibilities of life and their unwillingness/inability to overcome the obstacles that stand in the way. It seems like every time I get low enough to want to give up, someone or something reminds me of why I wanted to do this in the first place–it is the most pure form of self expression I have. So sometimes the reminder is praise. Other times it's the awkward mirror of my peers. But in the end I know I'll never stop creating something that expresses how I feel about the world I live in, and want to share that with other like-minded individuals.

In this crazy world, what is your best advice for a budding entrepreneur, artist, or innovator?

Be specific and singular whenever possible. Pay homage to (hell, wildly steal from) those who have influenced you for sure–but say something unique, personal and individual. As contradictory as it sounds, that's actually the secret to being universal.

Karin Elgai
STYLIST

> "It's like... Do you want a Christmas tree or
> do you want a puppy? ...What's going on?"

We met for the first time at Good Stuff Diner on 14th Street. It was a lunch, to see if she'd be interested in styling a photo shoot for my new record. I knew only a few people in the city at the time, and had reached out for recommendations. My wonderful friend, Kristen de la Renta had raved about Karin, saying I'd love her and we'd get along.

She was right. Like peas in a pod. About ten minutes in, we were giggling and kicking ideas around.

Karin has a gigantic personality. She is one of the most headstrong and hard-working people I have ever met in my life, and the work she has done to forge a career in New York City would floor anyone. She is the living definition of that tenacity people talk about when it comes to making it in the Big Apple.

Beyond styling, we became good friends, and I learned a lot about her story, which is not without a heaping helping of struggle, courage and daring choices. She has inspired me to be bold, which is a gift I am lucky to be able to pass on in this book!

~

What was your first job ever?

I was 14, before babysitting. My very first job at a workplace was at a pizza place. I was the counter girl and later on I was in the kitchen. I was cooking.

You're kind of a foodie!

I'm a huge foodie. I've been a cook in five restaurants including the pizza place. I have a huge relationship with food.

Talk about how you felt when you graduated high school...versus how you feel now about the question "what do you want to be when you grow up?"

I did not graduate high school! I was extremely concerned at the time because not only did I not graduate, which I was sure would slow me down, I didn't serve in the army. So, in Israel when you don't serve in the army a lot of workplaces would not hire you because you did not serve the country, and it's mandatory, and you're a moocher, pretty much. So, as soon as I could, I left Israel. I did not like it there. It made me feel really, really dark. You're constantly surrounded by news reports that make you depressed. I came to NY in 2007 for a month and checked out some universities, and I promised myself that, if I would be able to save the money and move here a year after, I would. One year after, to the date, I was in New York.

If you're bound for greatness, you'll find it one way or another. All they tell you in high school is that if you are not going to show up to class and be behind the gym smoking, then you aren't going to amount to anything. If you're stubborn enough to want something, and hungry enough to get it, then nothing can really stop you.

What were you hungry enough to want?

To be awesome (laughs).

What do you do for a living?

Fashion, prop and set styling. I'm in charge of building a vision with the photographer. Let's say it was an editorial that was not an assignment from the magazine. We'd have to have a discussion and work out a concept, a vision and theme. Once that theme is gathered, we would put together some reference images as to what we want the lighting to look like, the make-up, the clothes, the fabrics. Then I would contact the showroom and do my research about the current collections and future collections and try to bring it all together and try to make it look fucking incredible.

It's a far cry from "being concerned" about not graduating! A lot of people would not dare to go out on their own.

My parents were really concerned, but they got an advice. My mom's a hairstylist. She has a salon, and one of her clients gave her advice to let me be and that I will amount to greatness. She calmed them down. They just let me make my own mistakes. They're incredible parents. They've been very supportive. I was free to make my own decisions about being rebellious. So, as soon as I finished high school I moved to Tel Aviv for my own apartment when I was 17. Two years after, I moved to New York!

What were some of the biggest challenges of coming to another country, leaving behind your network and trying to make an impression in a new place?

Who I was in Israel and who I am in New York is completely different because I'm completely demented. I'm crazy in the head. New York is way more open to that. So, what I would call temporary friends back in Israel...they would be friends with me for about six months and then they would get exhausted with my bullshit. Here, [I have] life-long friends who have just the same bullshit issues, and are just as crazy as I am and we all embrace it. We're there for each other and it's amazing.

The biggest challenge is probably selecting your dreams. Let's say I say no to a job. There are a million stylists, and a million photographers, and a million graphic designers and a million makeup artists. They don't need me; they would do just fine without me, so making your mark in the industry... I still haven't, and it's really hard and I would love to do it. I would really like to do something that would blow people away.

What is the worst "cry yourself to sleep at night" failure that you experienced–one that you thought would tank your career, but it didn't–that stands out in your head?

Well, our good friend Natalia has said to me a lot of times when I would cry myself to sleep...she said, "brush it off," and that stayed with me. I don't take it as that big of a deal anymore, but...

I did have a time when I was on set with a client. She was an up-and-coming jewelry designer. She could not afford my full rate so I gave her half my rate. While on set, she did not give me any references as to what she wanted so I had no idea what I was coming to do, and she just started messing with my styling and breathing down my neck. At some point during the shoot she invited her friend to style her jewelry, when I was called in for the job. I found that very disrespectful. At the end of the shoot she told me she was only going to pay me half, and I told her you're already paying me half - I cut down my rate for you, I came in for the full day, you don't know what you want, and you're gonna pay me the full price. She tried to give me a check and I was like, "no, no... I'm gonna need cash."

I left, and I came here, actually, after the shoot and drank my feelings away because I was just beyond furious. So furious. I didn't think it would tank my career, because there was no career just yet, but yeah. Stuff like that makes me very frustrated—when a client doesn't know what they want and you just want to show them the back of your hand, and just shake them and get answers out of them. It's like... "Do you want a Christmas tree or do you want a puppy? What's going on?"

What was the best experience that was eye-opening or... it just went perfectly and you thought "this is what I'm meant to do"?

I had a week when I was booked for two last minute jobs. I was booked for costume design for a short film, and I was supposed to build five sets and style five celebrities for GQ. When I first started, my dream was to style for GQ, and after that my husband asked me, "So you got to the dream! What's next?" and I said, "Well I'll just have to find a new dream." He said, "Well, what would that be?" and we were watching the Oscars at the time, and I said, "I'm going to win an Oscar for costume design!" So that's next. Talk to me again in a year!

You're doing exactly what they say to do: have a goal ...and a set of incremental goals that gets you to the big goal ...and then know what meeting the goal would look like. So you know if you hit it...

Well, that's the thing though. I didn't decide that styling for GQ was a short-term goal... I thought it was probably eight years from now. You just gotta keep pushing. My first two years in New York I worked for free, which I hated doing, but I didn't know as much as I do now. So people would ask me to work for free all the time. It's frustrating, but unfortunately it's the industry standard, and you've got to learn somehow. After doing this for a few years and starting to build my contacts and my business, and now I have people from FIT, from the styling program I did there, contacting me on Facebook, asking me to give them consultations and asking me to give them advice. They were way better than me when we went to FIT, but they didn't keep at it. You've gotta stay super hungry.

You're really good at getting out there and hustling for your work... How does that feel? Is it exhausting? ...Exciting?

Not doing anything makes me exhausted. I'm very much prone to depression, so if I'm home for just one day and I'm not sending out invoices, on the phone, looking for work, emailing agencies, I get sooo down. Work is my drug. I love it. I love what I do, and I love to keep it busy. Not working is not an option for me.

Are you motivated by challenging experiences like the one you had with the jewelry designer?

Absolutely. I love that I had it because it can't all be peaches and berries–I love peaches and berries! In Weight Watchers those are 0 points! Give me peaches and berries all day...but...It can't all be good.

My parents told me once... We used to get allowance as kids, and it wasn't too grand, but we got it every week. And one week we didn't get allowance. My parents told me it was because they hadn't made much money that month. My mom has the salon, and it depends on the business coming in and out. I could not comprehend it...like "What do you mean I'm not getting an allowance?" They told me that I have to accept that "no" is an option sometimes, and you have to accept the word "no." So, "no allowance" is not the end of the world, and "no something else" is not the end of the world. You have to go through bad experiences in life and brush them off. See what it is.

I'm glad I had bad experiences... It taught me how to deal with clients later on. Someone asked me if I am good with dealing with bitchy clients. I don't have bitchy clients. Some of their requests are difficult, but they are all trying to get somewhere.

You can't treat your client as a negative source because: who would want to be your client? All my clients show such appreciation. When I was doing that job for GQ, I was in the studio from 9am to 10:30 at night building sets, and painting, and moving stuff around and hanging Tiffany lights, and the next day that was work that I would have been proud of even if I had two months to pull it off. So, the fact that I've done it in a day is just ...I can't fucking wait for the next time that someone drops something on me that's like "you have 30 seconds to make this and you get something awesome out of it".

So, you get an adrenaline rush when you have the extra challenge...

Exactly. One of my first jobs, I was doing costume design for this music video and they changed the storyline throughout the shoot and they wanted a wedding. They wanted a bride and groom scene which was not in the original script. So, I took the bed sheets from the scene that they shot before, and I draped them on the director because they didn't cast anyone to be the bride. So, the director volunteered and she was fabulous. I think it's in my blog, that story; it took ten minutes, three safety pins, two double sided tape and a rubber band! We had a wedding dress!

Is there a specific piece of advice for a new artist entering into the world trying to make a living.

I would probably say what I tell my husband which is... "Don't stop. Oh God, don't stop." (laughs) You have to keep going.

Someone told me that about my diet; I'm in Weight Watchers. We were talking about how there's this thing... this feeling that if you slip in your breakfast, you would not care about the rest of your day, so you would eat a shitty lunch and a shitty dinner, and kind of give up on that whole week, and maybe not show up for a meeting. So, someone told me "if you trip on one step, would you throw yourself off the entire flight of stairs?" So... you wouldn't! You would brush yourself off and you would climb on up.

People kind of need a fresh place to start... like I'll start my diet tomorrow, rather than my next meal will be better. They need the first of the month, the Monday, the Sunday...the beginning of stuff. But, what made my business what it is... is the fact that I have spent an obsessive amount of time on getting my shit together and reminding clients that I'm there, and just never, never, never stopping. Don't stop work. I take my iPad with me. I have a weekend in Pennsylvania with my husband coming up, and my work is coming with me there. It's our anniversary weekend and I'm going to be writing down photo credits. Don't let yourself get bored or frustrated.

You can always ask for help, which has been amazing for me. I was not shy asking for help from other stylists... like "Oh, I need the contact for Dior, could you maybe give me the email of the person there..." and some stylists have been incredible, and others not... because I can understand how you can feel threatened ...by how amazing I am (laughs), but some stylists have been incredible. I don't want to compete with mediocre stylists. I want to compete with amazing stylists and I want to win. Otherwise, it's no competition.

Sage Francis
MUSICAL ARTIST & RECORD LABEL OWNER

"Chuck D came to my table and asked if he could join me. I nearly choked on my food. I was no longer just the fan but a participant..."

Sage and I go way back to 1999. We met through the poetry scene in Providence, RI. I was an avid competitive poet in high school, and as I made my first foray into city living as an adult, it was easy to fall into the familiar arms of the poetry world. At the time, it was thriving, the poet community was tight, and we haunted all the great coffee spots, talking word-craft, life and passion - and for readings.

I first saw Sage at a slam (judged performance poetry/spoken word competition)... he was slinging styles I had never heard before. His work was good. Different. New.

We first talked at one of my quirky music performances at Cafe La France, and conspired to meet up at Ben & Jerry's just off the Thayer St. drag in Providence. I don't even like ice cream, but there we were. We made fast friends... and shared a lot of commonalities; northern mill towns, a love of words, complicated up-bringings, losses, personal drive. He introduced me to underground hip hop, DJs and to many people who are still my friends today.

In early 2000, Sage did something I both hated at the time and respected over time. He left. He went to New York and roughed it like some kind of Bob Dylan maneuver. It was the necessary push. He didn't have money. He slept on floors. All that stuff. It was something I wouldn't be ready to do for literally another decade.

Unapologetically, the guy just never quit. He built himself into an enigma and created an unpredictable, volatile character with alter egos, slogans, aliases and the works. Lots of people got hurt, and lots of people got entertained. But ultimately, Sage made a slew of strong, decisive moves, and he did his time on the road, then built an uncompromising business around his creative work.

We've stayed in touch over the years, and periodically checked in. He's been a good friend, and I am super grateful for the opportunity to share a rare bit of his candor with you in this book.

~

What was your first job ever?

I delivered newspapers as a kid. That was my first paying job. And then I delivered newspapers after college. I went through a slew of odd jobs until my music career started paying the bills.

Talk about how you felt when you graduated high school versus how you feel now about the question "what do you want to be when you grow up?"

I felt relieved that I would never have to deal with that school or group of people ever again. I was very excited to go to college so I could get away from my small, homogenous town and interact with different types of people.

Now, sadly, all I want to be when I grow up is left alone. Haha. Or maybe figure out how to regain that enjoyment I once had while in the company of others rather than just becoming more and more comfortable in my solitude.

What do you do today to make a living?

I run a record label, perform on stage, and sell music along with other music-related merchandise.

Describe the worst moment of failure in your creative/entrepreneurial career.

My biggest fail was the worst business decision I ever made. I signed over the rights of an album (in perpetuity) to a foreign record label I knew little about. They were not really equipped to handle the project properly, and I'm not so sure they intended on doing so, but I went into the deal based on blind trust. Hindsight is 20/20 obviously. It's tough to think straight when you want to keep the ball rolling and you're caught up in too many moments. A lot of artists make bad business decisions early in their career because you can't understand the full magnitude of what it is you're signing away. You're just excited that someone is interested in what you do and you want to believe they're there to take you to the next level. If and when you figure out that's not the case, there's little room for retribution when dealing with a "company" that exists on the other side of an ocean. Haha. Regretted my decision almost immediately, and that's something that continues to gnaw at my spirit. Needless to say, I'm more than cautious when signing dotted lines these days.

Describe the best success you've experienced in your field.

It was at the Rock the Bells festival in 2006 or so and it may have been in California. All I really remember is that I was sitting at a table all by myself in the catering area. Chuck D came to my table and asked if he could join me. I nearly choked on my food. Public Enemy was my favorite group growing up and definitely one of my greatest influences. I saw PE open up for Run DMC at the first music concert I ever attended, and I've been a diehard fan ever since. Anyway, I obviously told Chuck it was OK for him to join me at the table and I did my best to keep my composure as I introduced myself to him. He said he knew who I was and that he's a fan of what I do. That's why he wanted to sit at the table with me. Huh. Mind explosion. Scattered bits of brain all over the catering tent. We chatted about music and, to be quite honest, I don't even remember what else. Life had gone full-circle at that very moment and it was making me dizzy.

What's the connection?

If I had to connect the two, I suppose they both helped me reach some form of acceptance as to where I'm at in life. No longer just the fan but a participant in what was so magical to me as a kid. No longer blissfully ignorant to the darker sides of the magic. I'm all grown up.

Did you ever think of quitting or giving up, and more importantly why did you keep going?

I keep going because that's all I've done. This is the one consistency in my life. I became married to my career long ago and I've sacrificed too much to just let it all go away. However, I'd like to go off the grid at some point. I think about doing that often. If I can figure out how to do so without it negatively affecting other people in my life or in my company, then I probably will.

In this crazy world, what is your best advice for a budding entrepreneur, artist, or innovator?

I am asked this question all the time, and I've decided that the best advice I can give is for these people to read Bukowski's "Don't Try" poem.

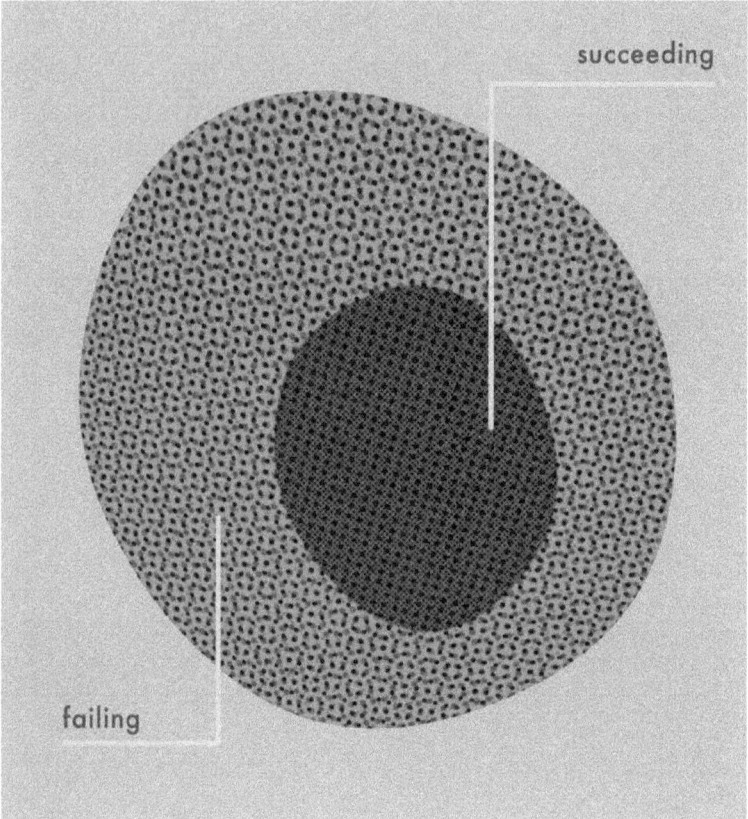

succeeding

failing

© 2013 Serena Andrews

Scotty Grabell
SCOTTY THE BLUE BUNNY

*"When people say be patient, they
don't mean 10 minutes. They mean 10 years."*

Back in the early oughts, I lived in an arts space in the heart of Providence, RI, called AS220. At the time, there were two galleries, a performance area and bar, a dark room and screen printing room, and on the 2nd and 3rd floors, there were work and live-work studios. I was one of the eleven artists living on the third floor. One of the studios up there was always reserved for an artist in residency.

That's how I met Scotty.

He brought an energy to the space that was new and awesome to me. I'll be honest, I was pretty weird, but this guy... he had taken weird, strange, fantastical and brave and just owned it...and put sparklies on it...and ears. Not only was he hilarious, but he did many things, both organized and subtle, to bring the community together. He hosted a "stitch and bitch" and participated regularly in the variety shows and other local theater. At the time, I remember he was part of this troupe called the Bindlestiff Family Circus. I was always in awe of his work.

As housemates, I was lucky enough to share some wonderful discussions with Scotty–some over drinks, some over breakfast at the Downcity Diner alongside a motley cast of AS220 characters.

When his residency ended he left a bunny-shaped hole in the place. Over the years, it has filled me with a kind of satisfaction every time I've looked him up, and there he is! He never stopped being himself.

I feel honored that Scotty took the time to be part of this book, and excited to share with you a glimpse into his world…

What was your first job ever?

My first job was as a cashier for Pathmark Supermarkets in Spring Valley New York. I wish there was more to say about it, but being a cashier in a supermarket doesn't really need much.

Talk about how you felt after high school versus today on the question "what do you want to be when you grow up?"

It's funny, but now that I'm 46, I don't even reference that time. It's numb, null, void. I'm old enough that I could have asked myself that question when I was 30, 40, or even last year.

As an artist there are these great moments of validation, security, and confidence, and then there is this return to a launching off point. I think even traditional careers go through that, where you go through a particular job, and then it's time for a move, lateral or otherwise.

If I could characterize it, I would have to say that because of being gay and being in the closet - high school was like walking around in a daze. Some kind of self defense fog. Now that I've been a rabbit for almost 20 years, I know I'll be brave and take pride in the risks I've taken.

I think to answer the question "what do you want to be when you grow up?" is the first pitch of a shovel in your grave. Never decide. Stay curious, keep working. That's what keeps you young and in touch with the world.

My mission now is to be an older glamorous person.

What do you do today to make a living?

I perform as a "character," Scotty the Blue Bunny in a wide range of events and presentations, and I also teach Pilates mat classes.

Describe the worst moment of failure in your creative/ entrepreneurial career.

Well, as with any job, oversleeping can happen in the arts too. I got confused on a booking and woke up all excited about a gig and contacted the woman through email with questions like what time should I get there etc. She replied, "the gig was last night". My penis went all the way inside my body, I was so embarrassed!

Flaking on a gig, like totally missing it, for someone's special 50th birthday party who specifically requested you to jump out of a custom-made cake...that was pretty bad.

Describe the best success you've experienced in your field.

It's difficult to say, because there are sooooo many different kinds of experiences from birthday parties (when you don't forget them) to corporate events, bondage parties.

I would have to say the most treasured thing I have is hosting 10 years of the opening gala for the New York Burlesque Festival. It's nice to have a decade long mark in the career.

How do you connect the successes and failures?

Well, at this rate, I say to myself "I've been performing for so long, and I'm going to keep performing. 99% of the time it's amazing. 1% can suck."

Even Madonna has bad shows. I don't go crazy about every performance because it's all so live. I'm not dancing or executing choreography.

I would have to say with the good and the bad - I just enjoy myself and keep moving forward.

Did you ever think of quitting or giving up, and more importantly why did you keep going?

It's too late. This is what I do. I think about quitting all the time. but What would I do? AND I really feel like I owe so much to past generations, and to all the glamorous people we lost to AIDS - that it is my duty, and my opportunity to be an older, out, gay glamorous person. We kinda don't have too many of them.

In this crazy world, what is your best advice for a budding entrepreneur, artist, or innovator?

Well, speaking to my field of theater–nothing you do on stage is frivolous. Everything you do has value. Every idea gets workshopped.

When people say be patient, they don't mean 10 minutes. They mean 10 years. When people talk about perseverance - they don't mean 10 minutes either. It's a lifestyle.

Robert Iafolla

FREELANCE JOURNALIST

> "...The thing about journalism is that
> it hinges on telling the truth."

We were in Miami. I'd been unceremoniously turned away at the V.I.P. room in the club we'd gone to. I was there with three girls, one of whom was a model, and the other two were dressed for the occasion. I had never imagined myself setting foot in a place like that, but I went in wearing what I had packed... blue and orange raver pants that zipped all the way up to the hip, sneakers and a shiny skintight teeshirt with multicolored Japanese characters on it. My hair was all pinned up in about ten twists with colored barrettes holding them in. I looked like Sailor Moon, if she'd become a career skateboarder. Needless to say, this was not within the dress code. So, I did what any responsible anime character would, and shuffled over to the main dance floor where all the boys were breakdancing and crashed that party. Yes. What you're picturing in your mind is correct.

I could only imagine the other ladies were getting free champagne and lots of attention in VIP, and they hadn't emerged yet. I took a break and found a balcony-type area where I leaned on the railing and hide out for a bit. Then, this guy (Bobby) came over and handed me a bottle of water.

Awesome!

That was thirteen years ago. Bobby and I have stayed friends ever since. It turned out he lived only a few miles from where I worked in Massachusetts, and was only in that particular club on that particular night because he was traveling on business. What an interesting way to meet someone!

I've had the pleasure of sharing countless hours of conversation with Bobby, ranging from political to family to fanciful to verging on purely academic. I remember when he first told me he wanted to be a writer, and he started doing articles for a local paper in Boston. I was thinking, "that's amazing!" I mean, he had a really cool job as far as I knew, and it seemed to be something that he was good at. But, I thought it was interesting that he just decided to make the change, then really did it. Now he does... what he loves!

Being freelance is a really tough thing to do... and being a writer for hire is something that I can relate to having been a freelance designer for a number of years. There's a definite art to selling something that does not exist... creating both the pitch to get the gig, and then the product from thin air. It's a little bit of witchcraft, so to speak. It's been awesome to know Bobby all this time, and to know someone that's stayed true to his craft!

~

What was your first job ever?

My first job was doing manual labor alongside my father during summer vacations during high school. One project was literally digging ditches. Among the myriad benefits of working with one's hands was, for me, figuring out that I wanted to work with my mind.

Talk about how you felt after high school versus today on the question "what do you want to be when you grow up?"

At age 18, the question of what I wanted to be when I grew up was an immensely abstract, existentially loaded notion that I preferred to avoid. I assume it's what a tenuously faithful Christian might feel if asked about what they'd want to tell St. Peter at the Pearly Gates. Now I look at growing up as a continual process that ends when you're in the ground & "what you want to be" as a question best answered by what you want to do.

What do you do today to make a living?

I'm a reporter, so I make a living by questioning, thinking, reading, searching, talking, detecting bullshit, and writing.

Describe the worst moment of failure in your creative/ entrepreneurial career.

I had been covering the U.S. Supreme Court for a small newspaper in California, but the paper decided to shutter its SCOTUS coverage to focus resources on California. Layoffs have unfortunately become an occupational hazard in journalism, but it felt like a failure just the same.

Describe the best success you've experienced in your field.

Getting that next gig certainly felt like great success.

Did you ever think of quitting or giving up, and more importantly why did you keep going?

I did think about changing paths, but I figured out what it is that I love about journalism and realizing that, at that point, not doing that was functionally impossible. While there are other fields that I could get paid for questioning, thinking, reading, searching, talking, detecting bullshit, and writing, the thing about journalism is that it hinges on telling the truth.

In this crazy world, what is your best advice for a budding entrepreneur, artist, or innovator?

It's best to figure out what fires your engine and understand what those things are in their most elemental forms. We have precious little control over our circumstances. But if you know what it is you're really after, you can maintain the flexibility necessary to get it.

Michael Kohl

GUITARIST, ARRANGER

"My vocal group got verbally trashed by Paula
Abdul...but in retrospect I laugh about it."

Michael and I met at a music pitch in Los Angeles earlier this year.
There were a few more than a dozen of us in the session hosted by
NARIP and we were pitching to music supervisor, PJ Bloom. Folks
played a wide range of musical styles and selections, and we all got
a chance to pick PJ's brain.

When Michael played his work, I think I awkwardly stared straight
at him. I'm no music supervisor, but I heard years of work, and
relentless attention to detail. It was pop music, heavy on the multi-
part harmonies. As an avid choruster in my school days, I was tak-
en sweetly back to a time when music was simply about singing.
(Today I do a lot of electronic stuff.)

After the pitch, we got the chance to chat, and the conversation
took a turn for the zany right away, from Sailor Moon to the ad-
ventures of rogue heart stickers. It was a great tension breaker,
because this was my very first music pitch, and I was outlandishly
nervous to be there.

Back in New York, I diligently followed up with folks I'd met over
the following weeks, and this was right around the time I was
putting this book together. With a little research, I could see he was
going on tour. What the heck. I reached out for the interview. So
awesome! BOOM! What a great addition to the mix.

Michael is on top of his game, and highly thoughtful in his communication. He pays solid attention to the little things, which sets
him apart personally and professionally. A little bit of polish goes a
long way, sometimes, especially if the thing you're polishing is of
good quality.

What was your first job ever?

My first job out of college was as an au pair. Yes, a male au pair... working under the table for a single mom trying to take care of her smart (but sometimes difficult) son while working a high-level job in the film industry with late hours. I'd wake up early to make him a bag lunch and walk him to school; later in the day I'd pick him up, drive him to gymnastics, cook him dinner, even read to him before bed. It wasn't glamorous but it had its own unique charms. And it helped me get on my feet, enabling me to save enough money to move out of my father's home.

I'll never forget my dad's reaction the day I got hired. I remember his proud face when I told him the news that I had a job, how loved and validated I felt when he extended his hand for a high-five... and how much it stung when he withdrew his hand after hearing exactly what job I had been hired for, and that other look on his face that replaced the proud one, the same I'm-ashamed-of-you grimace he gave me when we crossed paths at 6am as I was heading off to my employer's house each morning. My father was always an early riser, and I thought he'd be proud to finally see me getting up early too, to see me giving my all without complaint to work an honest job... it hurt me for him to be so open and consistent with his disapproval, but the money I earned working that job helped me move out and move on with my life.

Talk about how you felt after high school versus today on the question "what do you want to be when you grow up?"

When I graduated high school, my whole concept of what I wanted to be was based on keeping my options open. I knew I wanted to do something "big"--whether it was to be an actor, a musician, a famous writer, even a translator or diplomat. The biggest shift for me post-college has been realizing sort of the opposite: that, in spite of having many talents and options, if I want to succeed at anything (and live without regrets), I have to focus on a specific pursuit, really give it my all, both to maximize my chances of success and minimize my chances of bitterness in case it doesn't work out.

I eventually chose music as my career (at least for this stage of my life) because I noticed music was the one thing that, through thick and thin, I kept coming back to. I've had–and still have–many passions, but music is the one that I've always defaulted to to distract me from my other 'responsibilities'. And in return music has offered me an outlet and an identity.

What do you do today to make a living?

I began pursuing work as a professional musician full-time in 2010. Roughly a third of my paid work is as a session and contracted live singer, a third is as a touring and session guitarist and a third is as a writer/arranger, primarily for vocal ensembles (which is my specialty). There's very little overlap between those three categories, but I get to use all of my different musical skills in my passion project XY Unlimited, an original band that combines the soaring harmonies of vocal jazz and a cappella music with catchy pop/rock songs. XY is on the rise as a touring and recording artist and I hope to make that my main full-time pursuit as soon as possible.

Describe the worst moment of failure in your creative/ entrepreneurial career.

I think my biggest setback was in 2008 when a project I had invested myself in pretty heavily—a modern vocal jazz quartet called FourWest—suddenly disintegrated. I had formed the group with two fantastic young female singers I had fallen in with after college and with whom I had done numerous side projects. I thought I had finally found bandmates whose mindset (and talent) mirrored my own, so I was all-in, writing charts, setting up a network of players and planning a DIY tour of Japan. When they quit to pursue another opportunity with a group that had funding and a built-in administrative support structure (advantages I'd dreamed of having for a long time) it felt like the rug I had been standing on for two years was suddenly pulled out from under me.

They gave me a pretty transparently phony excuse about wanting to leave the ensemble in order to preserve the purity of our friendship, and I was left scrambling to replace them which proved futile because of the project's unique stylistic niche. In the blink of an eye, everything I had worked toward for two years was gone, with very little to show for it and no clear idea where to go next.

Describe the best success you've experienced in your field.

I think my biggest success so far has been forming my band. It started with a vision that came to me in 2009 of a group of guys that combined both the commercial viability and devil-may-care vibe of a modern pop/rock band and the boyish appeal and vocal arranging sophistication of college a cappella. I knew somewhere deep in my gut that I'd finally stumbled upon a direction after almost a year of floating, so I took a lot of time to flesh out my vision, come up with a plan for setting up the project and then execute each step--from arranging songs and producing rehearsal tracks to planning and running auditions to setting up an administrative structure and even a personal corporation to cover its affairs financially and legally. Today we're a touring act with a growing fan base and recordings I'm quite proud of, but I think my biggest success to date was in that beginning stage, where I was able to single-handedly transform my weird little idea from far-fetched brainchild to full-blown reality.

Is there a connection for you between the two?

Yes, most definitely. When FourWest broke up in 2008 an almost year-long process began for me in which I realized a hard truth: that I couldn't depend solely on associations or partnerships with other people as a primary source of realizing my own personal goals. Ever since high school I had always been the most hard-working, conscientious, driven member in any creative project I'd gotten involved in, and the result in each case had been some form of heartbreak. This latest disappointment gave me time to reflect on how all those projects I had invested so much hope into had ended, and I noticed that the problem rested with me and my expectations.

Meeting a musical partner can be like a promising new romance: you dote on your own notions of who the other person is and what they will bring to the table, and you imagine they see things the same way you do. But human beings are different from one another. They have different goals, values, boundaries, even levels of endurance. If you rely on someone else to serve as a vessel for the fulfillment of your innermost wishes, you're certain to be disappointed.

From that point forward I realized that, as unfair as it sometimes can feel in a world where so many people my age (or younger) seem to be ushered into success by being born into the right family or knowing the right people at the right time, if I wanted to get mine in this world I would have to do it myself, at least at first, and do it thoroughly, uncomplainingly and with wild resolve. Soon after, with a lot of careful planning and work in advance, I founded my band, a group that presents plenty of challenges of its own but is nevertheless alive and thriving after nearly four years.

This may sound cheesy, but looking back on the many things that have gone 'wrong' in my career so far leaves me with the feeling that it has all just been part of the process. Standing on stage in front of a full arena at the top final round of X Factor auditions in 2011 while my vocal group got verbally trashed by Paula Abdul felt pretty low in the moment—both humiliating and like an important opportunity was eluding me yet again—but in retrospect I laugh about it and mostly see the experience as something that has only tempered my resolve to keep moving forward. Plus, it makes a great story now.

As for the positive side of things, I think the biggest message I've picked up on is that conventional 'successes' are great, and worthy of celebrating and remembering... but ultimately fleeting. It doesn't take long for the high-on-life feeling after a successful CD release to evaporate in the face of some new challenge or inter-band conflict. That's why mental toughness is absolutely essential to having a career in any creative field. Successes (like failures) are great milestones, but you keep moving forward and before you know it they've faded into the distance behind you. You have to make the commitment to yourself that you're going to stick with it through the good times and the bad times, or you'll quit at the first (or second, or 415th) sign of trouble.

Did you ever think of quitting or giving up, and more importantly why did you keep going?

No, absolutely not. I'm a little crazy this way, because music might not be my most natural gift, and I still have a long way to go before I'm as 'good' as some people who are, like, half my age. I have no idea if it'll work out, and I've had hurdle after hurdle, frustration after frustration, disappointment after disappointment on this journey. But I keep going, because the one thing I do know--maybe the only thing I know--is that if I give up now I'll spend the rest of my life wondering, "what if?"... and that's a fate worse than failure.

Any advice for someone getting started?

The best advice I can offer to a budding entrepreneur, artist or innovator is to take your dreams seriously, no matter how far-fetched they may seem. And taking your dreams seriously means first identifying and exploring them, then coming up with a plan and seeing that plan through. And not being afraid to fail.

I recently read a great metaphor in a book by psychologist Meg Jay about professional uncertainty in your 20s. The analogy is that sometimes in life it feels like we're in the middle of a vast ocean, just treading water. As we move our arms and legs in the water to stay afloat, we look around us and, very often, see no sign of land or anything else in any direction. No birds in the sky, no sound of faraway seagoing vessels, no intuition in our heart to point us one way or another. And that's scary, because there's no hints, no structure, and no undo button. But in the end, you have to go in one direction and see where it takes you. I've learned that I'm not afraid of making mistakes; only doing nothing, that's what I fear. All my regrets revolve around things I didn't do when the opportunity presented itself, and all the good in my life has come from picking a direction and just trying it.

Mamiko Kushida

VJ & PROJECTIONIST

> *"I gave up my dreams...and studied law
> at university in Japan."*

I was at a small show in Bushwick. My friends Brian and Alex were each doing original electronic sets, and I'm a big fan, so I showed even though my date canceled. The music was great, as expected, but what blew my mind was there were these amazing images flickering and transforming on the wall. I felt transported inside of the mind of whatever artist had created it. I mean, I'd seen video projection at live shows before, but this was different.

When the show wrapped, I looked around for the projectionist area. I found Mamiko. I said that I really thought she could do this in big places and I wanted to introduce her to some of my DJ friends–it was amazing! She told me she she had moved to New York from Japan, and we switched information.

Over time, she has kept me posted about her work, and she is no amateur! It's been rewarding to watch as NYC catches on to her beautiful work.

Mamiko projects lush designs and iconic dancing imagery on customized surfaces in all kinds of 3D spaces...some of which are frankly enormous. She is not just a VJ, she is a craftswoman with light, color and space. At many of her shows, she actually builds the projection surfaces.

Besides her art, what impresses me about Mamiko is her humility and warmth in a city where that can be lost in the mix. I've seen her come out and support many other artists' work, which is the sign of a great friend and good character.

~

What was your first job ever?

I worked at a bank of Japan after I graduated from university in Japan.

Talk about how you felt after high school versus today on the question "what do you want to be when you grow up?"

I wanted to be a musician or illustrator.

I used to play piano more than 15 years and saxophone for 6 years when I was a child, and of course I loved to do illustration. It was very hard to get into art or music college in Japan (you must be very talented for art or music before getting into college).

I gave up my dreams to be an artist or musician and then I studied law at university in Japan. After I graduated from university, I worked at a bank. It was very easy for me to earn a lot money, but I felt something was lacking in my life. I missed playing music and doing illustration. I wanted to be close to music and art. It was then I made a decision to be an artist, especially VJ.

"I wasn't a wealthy artist but my heart was wealthy."

What do you do today to make a living?

I am a VJ and doing art direction for music events. Occasionally, I am a graphic designer.

Describe the worst moment of failure in your creative/ entrepreneurial career.

After a few years VJ experience in Japan, I came to New York.

I performed a lot of big music events in Japan where I got a lot of successful experiences VJing. But nobody knew me right after I came to New York. I didn't have any opportunities to VJ. I had to start to perform at small venues in New York. It was a very hard for me.

Describe the best success you've experienced in your field.

After my first year in New York, I got some opportunities to perform at big events.

I have been VJing for the world's top DJs (some Grammy nominated producers) such as Carl Craig, Jeff Mills, Derrick Carter, Frankie Knuckles, Easy Mo Bee etc.

Also, I've performed at the best clubs and venues in New York such as Cielo, (le) Poisson Rouge, Highline Ball room, Music hall of Williamsburg, Santos, Sullivan Room etc...

Is there a connection?

Yes, there is a connection. As I told, I didn't have any opportunities for VJing when I came to New York. But I had a confidence because I had already had some successful experiences of VJing in Japan before I came to New York.

I always imagined the successful experiences in Japan and I just believed in myself. I kept creating my art and being positive.

And then I got big opportunities in New York after a year.

Did you ever think of quitting or giving up, and more importantly why did you keep going?

Yes. I wanted to quit VJing in my early days in New York.

I spent a hard time but it was still my favorite thing. Being creative made me happier than working at bank which brought me a lot of money. I wasn't a wealthy artist but my heart was wealthy.

In this crazy world, what is your best advice for a budding entrepreneur, artist, or innovator?

I get inspired from a lot of great artists of the world, but I've never cheated anyone's art or idea. Cheating someone's art or idea is not yours.

You might be afraid of doing things which no one is doing. But you will find a right place for you.

Have your own style and be an original one.

David Madore

MUSICAL DIRECTOR, PIANIST, TEACHER

"Thinking back, I would have realigned my priorities to support my long-term career goals, and not to support my day-to-day living."

It was MSYM 1992–a sort of summer band camp held at the Orono campus of the University of Maine. There I was with a passel of girls, and we descended on the lunch room. David was across the room. He was this amazing pianist with a seemingly unlimited amount of energy. At the time he had coke-bottle glasses and braces.

I overheard him playing piano in the practice rooms, and I wanted to meet him. It wasn't long before we became friends. Later, in high school, we dated even though we lived a town apart. Music nerds unite!

It was no favoritism that led me to include him in this book. The fact is, David is ridiculously hard-working, and never took his natural talents for granted. All through school, he excelled in music and in his class work. Though we broke up for typical high school reasons, we have remained friends all these years. In 2010, when I moved to the city I was delighted to find out he lived locally and often worked shows and lessons on Broadway, right near my then apartment.

In my humble opinion, David has grown enormously, but his nature has changed very little... he is still thoughtful, silly, hard-working and a lover of puns. Additionally, he kept doing what he loves the most: music! I mean he really, really does what he loves, and keeps striving to do more, though not without the obstacles and difficulties of a very competitive and high-pressure industry and location.

I am proud and honored to share with you some of his thoughts on navigating Musical Directing and Coaching in New York, NY.

~

What was your first job ever?

My first job was when I was about 10 years old. I was hired to play piano at a church other than the one that I regularly attended (a different denomination).

"They're gonna pay me to go to church and play the piano?? SURE!!"

Talk about how you felt after high school versus today on the question "what do you want to be when you grow up?"

It has to do with your perception of your trajectory. Some of us are more introspective, or retrospective... but it's only when you get to the end of the path that you can go back and judge whether you stayed on it.

It depends on what you want to filter your self-image through. You can be facing the moon thinking that is your goal, when in actuality you're flying toward the sun–or maybe the other way around. You may end up doing something completely different than expected, look back and say, "Oh I've been doing this all along and didn't know it."

The truth is, I don't remember what I said I wanted to do when I graduated high school. I set out to become a teacher, and was drawn into musical directing in college, when I discovered that it existed as a career path. It turns out that musical directing is a form of teaching, among other things! It allows you to be a collaborative artist.

I certainly am that, and I certainly am a grown-up... but I don't feel like I'm a grown-up. I am always trying to more deeply ensconce myself in what I am doing.

What do you do today to make a living?

I musical direct, but I spend a lot of my time teaching private voice and piano lessons, as well as coaching actors on preparing repertoire and audition music.

Describe the worst moment of failure in your creative/ entrepreneurial career.

My worst moment of failure was when I chose to "move aside" as the musical head of a project, while working with some very caustic people, because I had been working a full-time (non-music) job, and had not been able to put in enough preparation time to instantly please those individuals. I am glad to say that my work to that point made all the difference in the quality of the actual performances, but it was certainly hard on the ego to not be standing there with the baton.

Describe the best success you've experienced in your field.

I musical directed and accompanied (on the piano) the actor Paul Sorvino in a classical concert series on the East and West Coasts. My favorite moment was when this movie tough guy started tearing up in the middle of an arrangement I'd done for him, and he later told me that I was the "best accompanist he's worked with in 30 years."

What's the connection?

The failure in one's life ALWAYS has helpful things to learn. Thinking back, I would have realigned my priorities to support my long-term career goals, and not to support my day-to-day living.

The success is a great thing on my resume, and the joy of the experience will last forever. I learned a lot by working with Paul, and would do it again in a heartbeat. It will certainly help inform my work in the future.

Did you ever think of quitting or giving up, and more importantly why did you keep going?

My current frustration is that I know and am "friends" with so many amazing professionals in my field, and have gotten very close to getting some jobs that I REALLY wanted, but have been passed over for other individuals who are a little more present in the eyes of whoever is hiring.

While I was married, I had very little support for my musical theatre career in the way it was needed. That led to quite a few years of being outside the business, and maintaining the oh-so-important PRESENCE that gets you connected and hired. Five years after the marriage ended, I'm still working to repair some of those missed career connections.

Every good coaching, every time I play for a singer, reminds me of why I keep going. It feels just RIGHT.

In this crazy world, what is your best advice for a budding entrepreneur, artist, or innovator?

Outlast your competition. Stick with it while the others drop out. Invariably, there is high attrition in the arts, in terms of those competing with you, and sticking around will eventually give you a higher experience level and better connections than those just starting out.

You must also work on your talent, and on making sure that your product, whatever it may be, actually has an audience. It's okay to make art/music that makes you feel good, but if it's not marketable or publicly consumable, you'll never make a living doing it. I don't think of this as "selling out" so much as honing your skills to find a better connection with the audience you are meant to reach.

Additional Note:
It seems, even though the work that I'm doing is incredibly time sensitive, and seems like an emergency... my feeling of capability doing those things is increasing. Suddenly there's a solution based on your experience. It's entertainment. Nobody dies if you don't do it well. You're not going to create a catastrophe.

Jeffrey Marriott

CASH HANDLER, CMO & COSPLAYER

"I am the geek that I've always been, and making a living out of it. What better success could there be?"

Even though I'd already met Jeff, I feel I really met him when I visited a coworker for movie night with friends. I had no idea they were roommates and was shocked to see him come downstairs in his pajamas.

Jeff is a sharp person, with a passion for negotiation, and I believe when we met he was telling the tale of successfully getting money back from a vendor. It seemed to be a point of pride, but after hearing the story I remember thinking, "man, if life hits the fan, I want this guy on my team!"

As with most of the people in this book, that is only one aspect of his talent, and negotiation is to Jeff what the Clark Kent disguise is to Superman.

Jeff is a wildly creative person, as well as being savvy, which strikes me as an unusual combination. It makes him a great resource for artists, and he sticks up for what's right.

~

What was your first job ever?

Newspaper Delivery Boy

Talk about how you felt after high school versus today on the question "what do you want to be when you grow up?"

When I graduated high school I was just happy to leave. I

didn't like high school, being a geek that was shunned and picked on a lot. When asked what I wanted to be when I grow up. I found it my opportunity to make people take a second glance. It was my time to shine, or just weird someone out.

What do you do today to make a living?

I currently work at Apple. Also, I am CMO for a small startup that focuses on K-12 education and keeping them in contact. Then I also consult for others with marketing and social media, I critique business plans, and one of my super passion projects, I make superhero costumes. Yes, superhero costumes. I always wanted to be a superhero when I grew up. Now I can be!

Describe the worst moment of failure in your creative/ entrepreneurial career.

I spent a lot of time and money building up a web zine for music when I was about 18. I maintained it for a couple of years and mostly just stayed afloat with it. However, due to some growth issues later and creative disagreements amongst partners, I chose to walk away from the project altogether. The reason I consider this a failure is that it was something I had a lot of passion for that I walked away from. I would've liked to have seen myself take a stand and resolve the disagreements a little more before giving it up.

Describe the best success you've experienced in your field.

Currently, I'm a freaking superhero!!! No really, I make super hero costumes. I currently make super hero costumes and at the same time manage an entertainer who travels the country dressing up as a superhero. I am the geek that I've always been, and making a living out of it. What better success could there be?

Is there a connection? If so, what is it?

Absolutely. I'm a huge believer in learning from mistakes. And I've wanted to walk away from what I do now, a lot. However, I continue to stick it out through frustration and this is what led to me being able to continue down the path I'm on. I'm very happy with it.

Did you ever think of quitting or giving up, and more importantly why did you keep going?

I constantly want to give up. But I don't. I push through and really evaluate if this is something that I'm unhappy with in life. If the answer is no and that I'm just frustrated at one detail of my life. I aim to change it. Ultimately, it has made me stronger and much happier.

In this crazy world, what is your best advice for a budding entrepreneur, artist, or innovator?

Do what you love. Seriously. Know that frustration will exists and you need to push through.

Barrie McLain

SINGER

> *"...Blaming the situation on others didn't cut it when my half-naked body was crucified five feet from my grandparents in the front row."*

Barrie is one of those people who lights up a room. I first met her at a training for a job. She was one of the facilitators. Creativity and passion blindingly radiated from her, and she was all smiles, even though we were just doing a routine orientation, and this was clearly a money gig for her. She was a beacon of hope that, rough edges and all, I might survive in a very structured environment with my own passions intact.

Shortly after orientation, the social networking requests came flooding in from all the new friends and colleagues at this behemoth institution. Of course, I did the obligatory "employee Facebook stalking" to suss out just exactly who my coworkers were, and what kind of lunchroom conversations to anticipate.

There she was... a singer! Ha! At that moment, I fell in love with Barrie as a concept, if you will.

Later, we did get better acquainted and it turns out we have a lot in common–she's been a singer for 12 years! Barrie's got a great story, which continues to unfold and shine. It wasn't a fluke back at that training... Recently, she made a career shift to focus more on her music, which most would consider a daring sacrifice of stability in exchange for flexibility. She gets her happiness from within, not from the externals, but knows when to take a risk and actively change a situation that that no longer serves her creative side.

My take-away from her example is that she delivers her A-game everywhere she goes, and keeps true to herself, above all else.

What was your first job ever?

I worked as an operator for rock walls and other carnival/ event equipment when I was 15.

Talk about how you felt after high school versus today on the question "what do you want to be when you grow up?"

When I left high school, I wanted to be in theater and music. I think more about when I was 10 years old and wanted to be an environmental scientist. I chose to go to a performing arts school instead to be closer to my friends, and since that decision the course of my life has changed entirely. Finding music made my life so positive and so connected. I want to be myself when I grow up, and music is where I am myself.

What do you do today to make a living?

I have a retail job where I spend most of my time supporting employee training. Often it feeds me artistically and I'm grateful to be paid for something I'm into.

Describe the worst moment of failure in your creative/ entrepreneurial career.

I starred as Jesus in an all-female JCS at NYU. I was under pressure and under-directed. The show was a disaster and ironically, it sent me into a cave. I learned a lot about what I need as a collaborator from that experience. Invasive demands were made on me as a performer during tech week and the production simply wasn't complete. I didn't have the skill to effectively communicate through the process and lost my way entirely. I couldn't ask the right questions or set boundaries, and blaming the situation on others didn't cut it when my half-naked body was crucified five feet from my grandparents in the front row.

Describe the best success you've experienced in your field.

My best success was a solo cabaret show I created during college. I sang songs that I love from ten different genres and met one of my very best friends and musical partners. It still effects my career and life regularly. Owning a process and bringing a team together to execute my own vision gave me great confidence and an opportunity to share my joy with an audience. I highly recommend it...and it reminds me that I need to get cracking on a solo project any minute now!

What's the connection?

There is certainly a connection in these extremes. To move forward with purpose one must define their own strengths and weaknesses, and also understand what is gratifying and what is not. The clarity of satisfaction in creating my cabaret stands in stark contrast to the murky discomfort of acting through a fractured vision.

Did you ever think of quitting or giving up, and more importantly why did you keep going?

I didn't decide to give up, but two years ago when I committed to my job full time, I put music in the backseat.

I sang backup for my friends, but I felt like I was shutting things down. There has been a part of me broken off and floating in space next to me, and it's fitting back together now. I'll continue for the love of my future children who deserve a happy, multi-faceted mother with 'following her heart' firmly under her belt.

In this crazy world, what is your best advice for a budding entrepreneur, artist, or innovator?

Keep doing it. One day you'll look around, and you'll realize how many people have stopped and let something more realistic or boring take them away, and you'll still be there. That's the best advice I've received as a budding artist.

Keith Munslow

MUSICIAN, CHILDREN'S PERFORMER, SHOW HOST

"... The sound system failed during the show, and someone actually streaked in front of the stage during the show."

I first saw Keith on the stage playing a mean piano with the Neo 90's Dance Band. The house was packed, and I was cutting a rug. It was one of the regular performances after the Pork Chop Lounge, a local comedic variety show. I was a huge fan of the show and the dancing after.

Little did I know, I'd eventually end up singing with that band, and joining Keith and cast in many iterations of his Empire Revue, the successful successor of Pork Chop Lounge.

Once I moved into AS220, we became great friends, and I even had a few piano lessons with him, hoping to absorb even a shred of what he does with left-hand bass lines. That had mixed results, but we've stayed close all these years. For a few years we both lived in "Whipple World", a privately owned collection of eclectic apartment buildings in Smith Hill.

Over the course of time, I assisted Keith often in his work as a children's performer, and did some graphic design projects for the Revue.

He has an extremely good reputation as a multidisciplinary artist, and his projects often succeed, but it's not an accident. He is a hard worker, and is passionate about building the community. They return love and support, in kind.

What was your first job ever?

I had a "job" at a local mom and pop store near our house when I was ten. I'd go in on Saturdays from 4-6pm and clean out the meat case, pack the meat in the freezer (the store was closed Sundays) and clean the sharp and menacing slicing and grinding machines. For this I was paid the sum of $6.00.

It was kind of scary, but I loved having $6.00 every week. I felt like a king.

Talk about how you felt when you graduated high school versus how you feel now about the question "what do you want to be when you grow up?"

I was sad when high school ended, because I had a great senior year. Not academically, but socially and artistically. I had a band and a girlfriend, and that seemed more important than anything to me.

I had a different answer every time someone asked me what I wanted to be when I grew up. Which is most likely why I do so many different things to cobble a living together now.

What do you do today to make a living?

I perform shows for kids and families at schools and festivals. My music for kids is played on Sirius, so that helps too. I perform with a New Orleans style swing band, and I am a teaching artist working in elementary and middle schools.

Describe the worst moment of failure in your creative/entrepreneurial career.

There was a show I was involved in with a puppet company that performed on a college campus. It was never really rehearsed, the sound system failed during the show, and someone actually streaked in front of the stage during the show. I was grateful for it, because it was a moment of comic relief in an otherwise dismal, disorganized disaster of a production.

Describe the best success you've experienced in your field.

Hearing my music played on Sirius for the first time and seeing my name on the radio screen in my car.

It was awesome.

Is there a connection? If so, what is it? Explain.

Failure keeps you humble. Success keeps you motivated.

Did you ever think of quitting or giving up, and more importantly why did you keep going?

All the time, especially now that I have a child to care and provide for. I keep going because I can't stop. Creativity is a force that is bigger than me. It drives me to make things and to collaborate with others. It is the gas in my engine every single day.

In this crazy world, what is your best advice for a budding entrepreneur, artist, or innovator?

Tenacity and adaptability are the two most important qualities to strive for. Making a living through your creativity, and by association as a self-employed person is certainly not for everyone. But the ability to wade through the hard times and challenges, and a willingness to be flexible will get you far.

Galen Richmond

"There's always someone who started a few years before you, and meeting those people and seeing their work is a great way to learn and be challenged."

Galen was wearing a yellow construction helmet. We were all sitting around on the lawn at the University of Maine. It was my first year of music camp. (See the chapter on David Madore.)

He offered to pay me for a book full of drawings and sketches I'd been working on. I was like, "No way!" ...and the whole bunch of our crew just kept talking about whatever. He and I never became super close, but we have stayed in touch over the years (mostly through social media).

In 2000, I went on a crazy tour with two girlfriends of mine. We looked for cheap or free places to couch surf or stay along the way. Galen kindly allowed us to stay at his house in Portland. We had a gig at Bull Moose Records and at a local bar down the street called Geno's.

I got a chance to briefly catch up with Galen at that time. He told me that he was in a band, and that he had been reading for audio books as a part of his living! How cool, I thought. That's one of those gigs people wonder about.

Periodically, I'd look to see what he was up to, or a post would appear in my Facebook news feed... Over the last few years, the posts have been about hacking electronics... as in hot-wiring toys and small electronics to access their sounds, and convert them into instruments. To me, as a fan of tinkering, this is totally experimental and interesting stuff!

I've never encountered Galen, or anything about him, where he wasn't making art and continuing to do his passions. He's a real gem, and I feel lucky to include him as part of the book!

~

What was your first job ever?

When I was 12 or 13, I mowed this colossal lawn a few times a week. It belonged to an eccentric friend of my dad who wanted certain areas mowed and others left patchy. There was a dilapidated school bus, a couple chicken coops and plenty of areas where the boundary between the lawn and the surrounding wilderness was hard to clock. Afterwards I'd chat with the guy for an hour or two each time. I was at the age where it was really a treat if an adult talked to you like a peer, so that was definitely the highlight of the job.

Talk about how you felt after high school versus today on the question "what do you want to be when you grow up?"

Well, I'm finding it doesn't get much clearer as you go along. Now, as then, "when I grow up" seems like a nebulous chunk of the future that I may or may not get to.

I guess the major difference between now (I'm 34) and when I finished high school is that, while I still don't know what it would look like if I got to a place where I considered myself to be grown up, I do have a rough idea what I'd like to accomplish in the next few years.

What do you do today to make a living?

Right now I tend bar while I'm in school for electrical engineering.

Describe the worst moment of failure in your creative/ entrepreneurial career.

I got this artist in residence position at the Maine Children's Museum, which seemed like a great racket.

I agreed to build them some interactive electronic stuff for the museum and to do weekly workshops, and it started off fairly well.

Quickly it became evident that I was in way over my head. I didn't have any of the tools, much less skills, I needed to fulfill my end of the contract. It was a horrifying summer, and I worked in a blind panic the whole time. I put in 40-50 hours for the children's museum in addition to my regular full time job. I stopped eating and was behaving pretty erratically from the stress.

Also, the kids just kept breaking my piece over and over and over again.

In the end, the project worked well enough. I did what I said I would, but really ruined myself in the process and nearly crashed my relationship as well.

Describe the best success you've experienced in your field.

There used to be this festival that happened every year in

New York called the Bent Festival, which focused on circuit bending and experimental electronics.

I went for the first time in 2007 and was beside myself with excitement to meet folks that were, within that small and specific scene, huge names. At the time, the work I was doing was pretty crude and it was a treat to get to talk with guys like Phil Stearns and Pete Edwards who were really making some beautiful and perplexing work with electronics.

At the same time, there weren't any musical performances that addressed my aesthetic concerns, so I decided that I would spend the next year building better instruments and developing a live set. I applied to the following Bent Festival, got accepted, and played a set that I was really pleased with. There was a complimentary blurb in the Village Voice afterwards.

Anyhow, I continued to play at the festival for the next few years, and eventually headlined the final Bent Festival and had an installation on display as well.

Ultimately, it was a small thing for a limited audience of enthusiasts, but I was happy to have had a clear goal and exceeded it.

Is there a connection?

Of course. The slow motion disaster at the Children's Museum made me pretty aware of my tendency to underestimate the amount of time money and work that goes into a major project. I use that as a metric now each time I'm committing to make something.

The modest success at the Bent Festival has put me in contact with some folks that are doing work in my field who are much much better at it than I am, which is super important. If you're working in a very narrow genre it's easy to think that you're this special snowflake and that no one is doing anything like what you're up to. But there's always someone who started a few years before you, and meeting those people and seeing there work is a great way to learn and be challenged.

The connection between the two, I guess, is developing a clear understanding of where you are in your process, what you can do, what you can't do yet, and what you'll figure out next.

Did you ever think of quitting or giving up, and more importantly why did you keep going?

No. I've made a few major changes of focus over the last 15 years, but I've never considered stopping.

It is fundamentally important to me to be passionately involved with some sort of creative work, and I get restless if I let too much time go by without getting into the studio.

And while I certainly haven't given up, I have changed what I want to accomplish. When I was in my early 20s, I was very focused on becoming famous and put a certain amount of pressure on myself in that direction. It was a great thing to let go of that (I'm not sure when it happened) and to decide that what I'd rather do is just make work that I think is good and true. If people see and like the things I'm doing, that's great, but I'm going to do it regardless and be happy doing it.

In this crazy world, what is your best advice for a budding entrepreneur, artist, or innovator?

Take some risks. Try a thing that's a little over your head and fake your way through until you get there.

Adam Rini

"Quitting would make me restless for the rest of my life."

When I met Adam, he was immediately likable. He made me laugh every single time I ran into him. Finally, I pinned it down to the fact that he could choose the perfect words and the perfect moment to speak them. In comedy, he never articulates those left-over ideas that tank the delivery. But here's the kicker... I never suspect it's coming! Even though my brain is thinking "Oh yeah, here comes that funny guy, Adam... he's gonna say something funny," ...without fail, he exacts ninja-like moves that render me useless for the remainder of the conversation.

I found out that he's an actor and film maker of 13 years, which makes perfect sense. He showed me some of the work he's done and I learned the story of his move to New York City.

Adam has a willingness to flow with the good that is happening in his life, without amplifying the bad stuff. For that reason, I felt he'd be a great person for this project.

He's struck a balance that I think a lot of artists fight for: the money gig/relationship/artistic work trifecta of excellence. If I had to guess why, I'd say he earned it, and if I had to guess how, I'd point to his attitude. He is way more than just a funny guy. You can tell when someone has heart.

What was your first job ever?

First job ever was part-time Ice Cream Slinger at a Tempe Dairy Queen. I was actually terrible at it. Ice Cream ruined both pairs of my shoes at the time. I was 16.

Talk about how you felt after high school versus today on the question "what do you want to be when you grow up?"

When I graduated high school, I thought everything would somehow work itself out. I had lucked and charmed my way through school and made the most of the opportunities that I had gotten, so I assumed that if I gave life about a 40% effort I would be just fine. I was a naive fool and wasted a few years floating through community college hoping for the best, getting high and playing video games. I wanted to be an actor and my fallback job was to be a philosophy professor. Typical stoner.

What do I want to do when I grow up? I want to be a creative full time. I want to work with and for people I trust and enjoy and I want to produce content for people I love and respect in ways that do justice to their art. I want to collaborate with challenging and fascinating artists who are more talented and differently talented than me. There are a million possible avenues that would fulfill the above qualifications. Specific examples include: writing, acting, editing, producing, or consulting for the projects in the medium of film, television, podcast, web series, or theater that have the potential to be sustainable or enriching.

What do you do today to make a living?

I am a cashier at a retail store, a freelance video editor, a non-union actor and videographer, speech and debate coach, film director. (Jobs listed in order of annual income.)

Describe the worst moment of failure in your creative/ entrepreneurial career.

The worst two moments of my creative life occurred in the same summer and are very closely linked in my mind. The security company I was working for as an overnight clerical specialist went out of business and I needed work. I took a role in a no budget feature as Captain Jack Tanner in "Star Quest: The Odyssey". They told me it would only be distributed in Germany and Japan. They also told me that we could play the terrible script as a campy comedy. In reality we shot a dead serious, laughably wretched sci-fi schlock film that ended up in every blockbuster and redbox in the United States. I still get hate mail for it. I used the $800 I made to make a web series that I was very proud of, and the lead actress accidentally destroyed the hard drive with all of the footage. So my sold my creative dignity for $800 and then I traded that $800 for a creative tragedy.

Describe the best success you've experienced in your field.

The greatest artistic success I ever had was doing a play at the New School for Drama in NY. I was not a student there but I auditioned against students and on merit I got the part. It caused a pretty big controversy but by the end of the show the teachers and the other students told me that we had pulled off something really special with the show and I met my wife during the run.

The most success I had professionally was a short film called "This Just In". It was a comedy about a news room made for Campus Movie Festival, a nationwide college film contest. We were a western finalist so that means we were in the top 16 of 20,000 entries and we were screened at the Cannes Film Festival, many Virgin Atlantic flights, and the IFC television network. Comedian Patton Oswalt watched it and said that it was "Very, very funny."

What's the connection?

I learned the folly of making work you know to be terrible, and the price you pay for trusting shady people you have never worked with. I learned that good work trumps all and at the end of the day, your reputation and the people who want to collaborate with you are your most potent currency. Be kind to your rivals and work with them if they inspire you.

Did you ever think of quitting or giving up, and more importantly why did you keep going?

Never. Quitting would make me restless for the rest of my life. People say "you never know if you will make it if you don't try." Fuck that, if you know you will make it you will try until you make it, come hell or high water. Even posthumous success happens. Never quit.

In this crazy world, what is your best advice for a budding entrepreneur, artist, or innovator?

Be kind, competent and helpful to everyone you work with; people who do not start well sometimes get much much better.

Be someone people trust and like to work with, and people will call you when they have work.

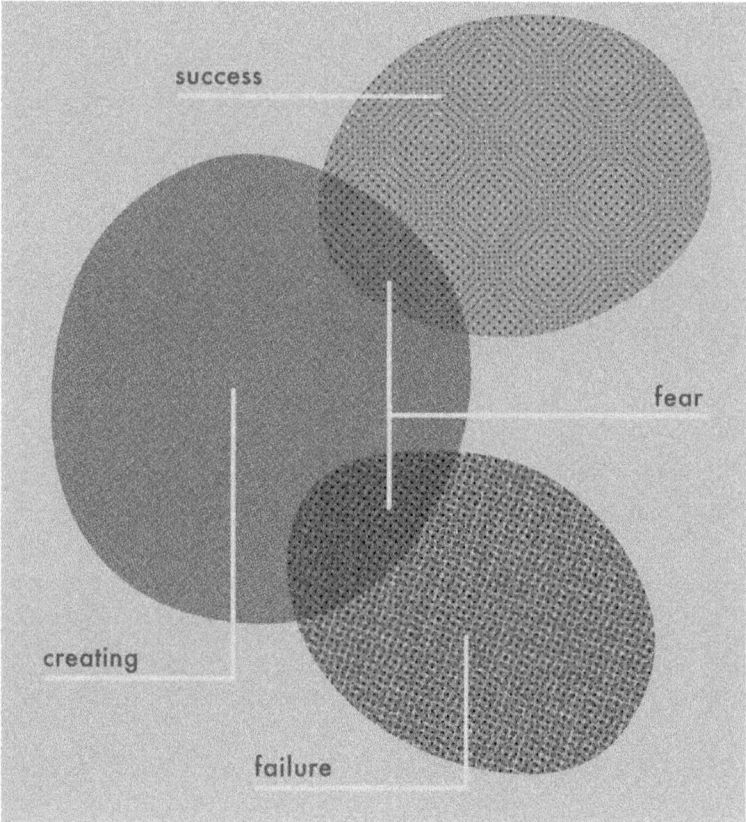

C. W. Roelle

"The errors stay with me as a sort of slap up side the head to work better. The successes keep the slaps from hurting too much."

I know him as "Sonny". He had a big turtle. I went into his room at AS220 to see the turtle, and noticed all these photographs and images from the 20s and 30s.

He was quiet and peculiar, but it was clear that he has a wry sense of humor. Over the years, I really got to see it come out via his musical performances and art.

Currently, I have 2 pieces of art made by Sonny. One is a print of many tiny wire sculptures, each of a different type of cheese. Black wire against a white background. It says CHEESE at the top. The other is a set of 3 tiny colored wire sculptures. I won these at a Christmas "blind gift swap". I was super lucky. You never know at those things.

Sonny is another person who marvels me with the ability to balance regular "straight jobs" and art. He is also supremely humble. Those two characteristics landed him on my list for the book. What a treat.

What was your first job ever?

Aside from short lived stints picking corn (2 whole days) or babysitting or mowing lawns or selling food tickets at the fireman's carnival my first regular job was working at Bud's Polar Bear which was an ice cream shop and diner. I was fifteen.

Talk about how you felt after high school versus today on the question "what do you want to be when you grow up?"

I knew I wanted to be an artist but I didn't know what that really meant or what art I wanted to make, I just knew I liked to draw. Now I know what I want to make and what it'll take to do it and I hope I get to one day.

What do you do today to make a living?

I just started a job as a rural postal carrier. It might be the most stressful job I've had as far as what needs to get done in what amount of time. It's only a few days a week though so I'm not totally burnt out yet. I was working in the mail processing plant before this for 5 weeks and that was 6 days a week and around ten hours a night and constantly moving and lifting and sweating factory work.

Describe the worst moment of failure in your creative/ entrepreneurial career.

Hmm, well there have been little failures. Plenty of those but no big blunders. Maybe showing up at a RISD summer program class to give a slide lecture and bringing an empty slide tray. Other than that it would just be investing more in a show or opportunity than was returned either in exposure or financial gain. Also not getting enough work done in time for a show which is a problem I face in two weeks.

Describe the best success you've experienced in your field.

I think the best show I have been in was at the long gone Space At Alice in Providence. I was given the space for a month (the last month it was open) and I invited 3 fellow artists (William Schaff, Jim Frain and Todd Watters). There were an estimated 600 people at the opening (though that seems a surprisingly high number). Another good show was one that I had in Baltimore also with Schaff at the (now also gone) Mission Space Gallery where through pluck and luck we had Will Oldham play music at the opening, which was also well attended. I was on a TV show once called Craft Lab on the DIY channel and that was fun (I went to Burbank to film it). I made a prop for a John Waters film back in 1999 (Cecil B. Demented–I made the branding iron). I was called down to the set at one point to redesign the piece so that steam could be piped through it. Of course, selling a piece is always a success and good reviews are nice things. Recently my work was the topic of a blog post on the website Colossal and many other blogs reran versions of it including Juxtapose Magazine's site.

Is there a connection?

Sure, the errors stay with me as a sort of slap up side the head to work better. The successes keep the slaps from hurting to much.

Did you ever think of quitting or giving up, and more importantly why did you keep going?

No, making artwork is all I really want to do professionally and though financial realities don't allow for that it remains the goal. But if I never sold another piece I'd still do it forever because, well, I like it.

In this crazy world, what is your best advice for a budding entrepreneur, artist, or innovator?

Stay away from debt.

Get to know as many people as possible in your field.

Get to know as many things as possible about anything.

Don't give up.

Be realistic.

Zac Sax

MARKETER, TEACHER, THINK TANKER

"Every project I've created has made me better;
...There's only growth."

I met Zac when he was maybe 14 years old. It was at the Hope Street Cafe, a staple poetry and music venue in Providence, RI.

He was familiar with my best friend, Elizabeth, and he was often there around the same time that I'd drop in for a coffee. We started out with a very adversarial and joking rapport. Zac had a sense of humor and capacity to play with sociological and psychological pivot points that was well beyond his years. I told him he would be an amazing businessman... he has the gift of gab.

Some decade and change later, I don't think he's really changed as far as personality goes. I was at Le Poisson Rouge in NYC just three years ago, and through the fog of the smoke machine we recognized each other. I think a mashup of DVNO and Madonna was shaking the place at the time. It was fitting that we'd both end up in New York at the same spot, and it's nice to see what he's been up to. Pretty cool stuff.

Zac stands out to me because of his rockstar attitude and tenacity for finding a fun and effective road to the results he wants. It seems he simply rejects anything that doesn't fit these criteria, but I'm sure it's secretly harder work than he lets on.

I hope you enjoy these sage thoughts from a charismatic upstart. I sure did.

What was your first job ever?

I sold suits at Syms in Rhode Island. It was cool, everyone else working there was in their 60's. I got a bunch of free suits and dressed like Bugsy Malone in high school.

Talk about how you felt after high school versus today on the question "what do you want to be when you grow up?"

Most people want to be something when they grow up and then disappointedly settle into something else that isn't really what they always dreamed of. I had the opposite happen: I had no idea what I wanted to do in high school; now, I couldn't dream of anything better than what I do.

What do you do today to make a living?

It's complicated; I do a few different things. First and foremost, I have groups of people who make stuff that can create a profit. The groups are comprised of writers, designers, developers, hackers, artists–whatever. We then work together to create something that'll either earn money or garner attention and PR.

When I'm not doing that, I freelance in advertising and creative as a copywriter. I've worked for a ton of ad agencies from Droga5 to BBH. It's fun, I mostly just sit in a room and think of ideas all day.

I also have my own fashion line, events company, and a small startup. And I teach all that to kids who want to do what I do at a graduate program in Brooklyn.

Describe the worst moment of failure in your creative/ entrepreneurial career.

I don't know if I ever had a 'worst failure.' I've had projects I hoped would take off and get more attention than they did, I had projects that didn't go through, I had projects that a client changed until they were nothing like they were intended. But I'm proud of all of them, I put everything I had into each and every one.

Describe the best success you've experienced in your field.

A couple of years ago I did a project called Underheard in New York with a few partners while I was at BBH. We gave prepaid cell phones to four homeless men and taught them how to tweet. They then tweeted what it was like to be homeless in New York- their thoughts, their feelings, their experiences. The reaction was amazing, people were responding to their tweets in real time, helping them and giving them anything they needed. The climactic moment came when one of the homeless men was reunited with his daughter, who he hadn't seen in over 13 years. Thanks to the help of one of our generous followers.

Is there a connection? If so, what is it? Explain.

Every project I've created has made me better; better at concepting them, better at producing them, better at publicizing them. There's only growth.

Did you ever think of quitting or giving up, and more importantly why did you keep going?

No. Every time I got even close to giving up per se, I would get frustrated with my plan B and decide that I was [going to make it work].

In this crazy world, what is your best advice for a budding entrepreneur, artist, or innovator?

There are two ways to do anything. There is the right way-this where you learn everything that came before you, study every aspect of the craft, build your knowledge and understanding, and see the path laid out for you ahead. You study it, understand it, and then improve upon it, making you the next in the lineage of great masters.

Then there is the wrong way. Where you do none of that, ignore everything and everyone, do what you want, follow nobody's advice, and just fuck everything by being so dramatically different that you boggle people's minds.

I highly suggest the wrong way.

Don Schlotman

MUSICIAN, DESIGNER, PUBLISHING ADMIN

"In the back of my mind [when I take a break] I know that I'm going to do it again. It's a bit like an addiction ...I get stir crazy. It's not really an option to quit."

I met Don at the PATH cafe in Manhattan. He was playing a mean guitar and singing with authentic punk irreverence. It was as if Tom Waits and The Talking Heads spawned a love child. Everyone at the bar said he was a great guy.

This was a regular open mic hosted by Niall Connolly, an Irish musician, and friend of Don's. After the music wrapped it turned out there was a plan to grab drinks. We all headed to a pirate themed bar just a short walk away, and Don and I ended up chatting. He is another multi-faceted person with his hands in a lot of different creative outlets and industries from publishing to music to painting and so forth.

One of the things I loved about Don's attitude right away is that he supports other artists and attends other events, which is a sign of solidarity and community building, in my opinion. He was a big promoter for several other musicians in the scene, and the takeaway feeling when talking to him is that he is "good people." The folks at the bar were spot on!

I think it's essential to be part of the community and get outside of oneself when making a career, no matter what industry or niche you're in.

I wanted to touch on the idea of being multidisciplinary with Don, so this interview is slightly different. I hope you enjoy it.

What do you do today to make a living?

Some copyright/permissions/research work for textbooks, some graphic design & art, some music.

Do you consider your art a success?

Yeah I do and I have had moments in my life when I have lived more on that, and others where I haven't.

I decided this year that it's a medium-term goal to spend more time doing art and music for a living. I have been working on more design clients.

I like the idea of having a separate job–it keeps me honest with my heart, so I don't have to sell out. Since I'm not dependent on it solely for my income I feel more free to do what I want to do.

Describe the worst moment of failure in your creative/entrepreneurial career.

I've had plenty of "failures"–the normal things like a small or non-existent audience, or worse, one that is not paying attention at all–but I try to not see them as failures so much as things which inspire me to improve my art and my ability to get an audience's attention. Usually a failure or ridicule drives me to create as much as success does, so I try to learn from it.

The worst... I went in to this gig and it was sort of crowded when I got there, enough to make me think it was going to be a great night. And very shortly after I started playing, the table in front of me got of up and left. It was sort of demoralizing because even my friends who stayed were talking so loudly that I could hear them over my playing. By the end of the night there were three or four people in there. A couple of people surprised me by saying they heard the music.

A similar situation: A lot of people in my family have never seen me play and about three years ago I went to a family vacation in Savannah, Georgia. I tried to use that opportunity to book a gig in Savannah while I was there. I thought it would be fun to play for my family. I did and it was fun, and it was actually really crowded, but right in front of me my aunts and relatives were having the loudest conversation.

Both of those experiences have made me work on ignoring that or powering through. It's still positive.

So, you used a service called Rocket Hub to crowd-fund the recording of your album Mother Transit Authority. How did you go about it?

I used Rocket Hub. It's similar to Kickstarter. One thing I liked that I don't know if Kickstarter does: if you don't raise your entire goal you still get a percentage of your money. It's NY based. I found out about it from some friends who used it. They were very supportive and helped.

It's a big choice to step out and ask people to put up funds on the merit of your idea and past work. What were some concerns at the beginning of your experience?

The obvious one… it had the potential to be disheartening if I didn't meet my goal and I don't like to feel I'm begging. I'm better at promoting my friends music than my own. It was challenging to feel confident that people would put money where their mouth is.

So you actually hit your goal. Describe how you felt at the end of your campaign.

It was nice. Elated. Some friends …one of them was still really excited that I was doing creative work and gave a nice chunk of money. She believed in the idea of wanting to support the art of friends. To her the amount might not have been that much.

One thing I like about the rise of DIY culture is that it democratizes creation, which is something that always existed throughout history. We're supposed to be active participants instead of just consumers. I like the fact that this is happening.

Do you feel both success and failure helped you in some way?

Definitely. Generally, I don't believe in duality. We are a product of every experience, good and bad, and often something which seems bad at the time leads to good things, just as good experiences can potentially make people complacent, lazy, or cocky.

Did you ever think of quitting or giving up, and more importantly why did you keep going?

I can't. I take breaks sometimes, but even then tend to still do creative things but in a different medium. For instance, if I am in a rut on the bass, I find that playing the banjo or guitar or keyboard can help, just as painting or building something can. When I come back I almost always have moved beyond whatever I was stuck on.

In the back of my mind [when I take a break] I know that I'm going to do it again. It's a bit like an addiction…I get stir crazy. It's not really an option to quit.

Talk about your thoughts multi-disciplinarians in our culture.

I guess our culture tends to think of things very linear. Instead of looking at the basic problem solving skills behind creative outlets including programming or math, I see them as related and like mental exercises.

I've never been a specialist. It's useful. I'll get mad about my guitar playing, and I'll paint or play bass then when I get back to it I realize I've had this breakthrough.

Keith Souza

"Success is when I wake up in the morning and
don't feel so crazy that I can realize
how lucky I am to live the life that I live."

Keith Souza is a supremely nice guy.

While I'd normally think that was a lame description, it's loaded
with meaning in this case. When I moved to Providence, RI back
in 1997, it was a strange journey getting to know who my crowd
would be, and where they would be. In the early oughts, I felt like I
was finally meeting some cool folks. That was when I lived at the
AS220 artist studio spaces, and started to really explore the less
obvious things to do around town... Providence hadn't totally bust-
ed out into full-on Hipsterism yet, though it was well on its way.
Today, at a surface glance, I think it would easily compare to San
Francisco, Austin, or Williamsburg in Brooklyn.

By 2007, mustaches, tattoos, microbrews and kitsch appeared to be
in full swing, and for all intents and purposes, I could easily have
been lumped into the Hipster category, along with most of my
friends, and plenty of other innocent people with great ideals, good
ideas, and a love for their craft and community. However ironic it
may seem, and therefore condemning, I never really felt that I was
fully included in the trendy groups. I had a ton of friends from the
restaurant and arts industries, and I'd met a lot of people in a
decade, but I sort of held a certain circle of folks in this very exclu-
sive space... Keith was one of these people - owner of Machines
With Magnets. Looking back, the whole notion makes me laugh a
little because it was based on a whole lot of assumption, and hap-
penstance. I simply never had the chance to meet Keith on a casu-

al social level. I've since become close with several people from said circle, and have eaten my words. And I met him. Absolute sweetheart. Really cares about what he does.

When I finally had a conversation with the guy, I thought about it for about a week. I guess what I felt was a bit ashamed that I had fallen into the trap of clumping together trendy and artistic people that were doing something I didn't feel part of into a stereotype I'd been accused of embodying, myself! Haha. How's that for ironic.

Unbelievable bands had recorded at Keith's studio... and its reputation precedes the crew that work there. Machines With Magnets became a sort of institution, recording a wide range of bands, mostly artful and unsung groups with odd names and cool music that has an edge.

If you're ever passing through Providence, look the place up and drop in. You will not regret it, and you'll meet some fantastic people!

~

What was your first job ever?

I was a roofer with my grandfather when I was 16 years old.

Talk about how you felt when you graduated high school versus how you feel now about the question "what do you want to be when you grow up?"

It's hard to remember how I felt when I graduated high school. I was only 16 because I started school early. I was playing music. I was going to college because it was what I was supposed to do, but my heart wasn't in it.

I think the question "what do you want to be when you grow up" is a nice exercise for a kid.

What do you do today to make a living?

I run a recording studio and an art gallery/performance space with a bar. I am part owner of the building in which they reside. I also play music when I can.

Describe the worst moment of failure in your creative/ entrepreneurial career.

This is a difficult question. I wish I had some dramatic and interesting story, but the truth is the failures are a constant. I've lost projects and felt like a failure. I feel like a failure every time I do my taxes because I don't make as much money as "successful people". I've felt trapped, lost friends, had failed relationships. Starting and maintaining a business can take a toll. Living outside the normal routines of life can be a struggle and some people can be very unsympathetic.

Describe the best success you've experienced in your field.

The successes are also a constant. I'm sorry if this is boring. I've recorded successful records that have gotten great reviews. I've recorded amazing records that have gotten terrible reviews. I've had amazing shows at our space. I've met incredible people. I've made friends. I have wonderful people helping me. It's hard to pin any one thing down.

Success is when I wake up in the morning and don't feel so crazy that I can realize how lucky I am to live the life that I live.

Is there a connection? If so, what is it? Explain.

I know it's cliché, but failures and successes both help push me forward. Sometimes I wish the ratio between success and failure was a little different, but I don't think I would know what to do with myself if I was rich. I'd be willing to give it a try though.

Did you ever think of quitting or giving up, and more importantly why did you keep going?

I'll be honest. I do think of quitting or giving up sometimes. Who doesn't? Sometimes I think to myself "Who the fuck do I think I am making music for a living?" Sometimes I think it's irresponsible because I have no financial security. Sometimes I question its importance in the world, or even my own.

I keep going because music and art are important even if our capitalist society doesn't recognize it or if it does, it treats it with the same blind and thoughtless inequality that it treats most things in the so called free market. I keep going because I believe in what I do more than I believe in our economy or the standards that have been set by it. I want to conquer it. I want to prove the naysayers wrong. I can't picture myself doing anything else. I love what I do. The feeling I get from creating something is a feeling I don't want to lose.

In this crazy world, what is your best advice for a budding entrepreneur, artist, or innovator?

Make sure you believe in what you're doing and do the best version of that thing that you can possibly do. Lose the ego. Don't be afraid or too prideful to ask for help or to collaborate. Know that sometimes you have to work for free, but don't undersell yourself. Try to stay healthy. It's hard sometimes.

Kelly Walsh

"Not long ago I asked my parents what they wanted to be when they grew up. They both said they didn't know. They are only in their 70s so they have time."

Kelly and I met at her family's business in Providence, RI. It was a little underground restaurant and music spot in the swankier part of the East Side. I was a busgirl.

When we discovered that we both played music, we resolved to meet regularly and work on our songs together. To some degree we followed through with this... learning each other's harmonies and complementing piano/guitar parts. Honestly, I think it ended up being half therapy for me. I was going through a pretty rough time, and Kelly's kind ear and real friendship was a balm.

Though the rehearsals sort of fell apart, we stayed friends and a few years later, we (along with another musician, Christine Hajjar) decided to book an East Coast tour together. The plan was to travel from Bangor, Maine to Miami, Florida and back. We did cafes, bookstores, radio stations, oddball gigs, clubs and so on. Like some kind of singer-songwriter Voltron, we performed as one act, trading sets to make a full hour of music. We traveled in Kelly's green Saturn sports coupe, which was full of merchandise, gear and more shoes than were probably necessary.

This tour bonded the three of us very closely, and now whenever we talk it's as though no time has passed at all. Kelly has been a total inspiration to me because she started doing her passion of music at what was considered (in the late 90s) to be an older age. She simply didn't care. She wanted to do something that she loved, and so she learned guitar and went on to write a gorgeous and honest body of work. Her songs are well-written, and she has a true following of people who love her as an artist and a person. Besides that, she navigated a series of big ups and downs in her life, and has remained collected throughout.

Kelly embraced her involvement in her local Block Island community, and has deeply explored the practice of Yoga, as well as small business ownership there and online. I am just catching up with Kelly now, and she remains a seriously awesome example of how to live out one's dreams and ideas naturally and without too much drama. She did this all when people around her might have said she was crazy to "start over" or try something new. I just know that she's inspired more people than me, because she has done what people don't dare to do. She takes risks and doesn't listen to the naysayers!

With big love, I am super happy to share her interview with you here. I think you'll see what I mean.

~

What was your first job ever?

My first job was a paper route. I bought it for $30 when I was 10 year's old. I had my first taste of delivering goods and providing a valuable service. I had to be disciplined and organized. My parents both worked so the responsibility of the job was all mine. There was no such thing as them driving me around so I could make some easy money. I have heard of some parents doing this and it never made any sense to me.

Living in New England, I often had to deliver in rain or snow. When it snowed I would hook my dog up to a toboggan to help drag the papers around my neighborhood. Every week I had to bill my customers via an envelope left at the door. Sometimes the customers would "forget" to pay so I would have to keep a list of them and use my budding detective skills to identify when they'd be home so I could "shake them down" for the money. It was a challenging job and I took it seriously. The toil was all mine and I was proud of that.

Talk about how you felt after high school versus today on the question "what do you want to be when you grow up?"

I graduated from a high school in Connecticut where almost everyone automatically went to college. I did not want to go to college and had no idea of what I wanted to be when I grew up. I was so wrapped up in my life the way it was with all my friends that I could not think beyond it.

My parents told me I had to go to college so I half-heartedly applied to a few. My SAT scores were not very good. I was smart but I did not apply myself in school. I was not inspired or motivated by my teachers. Like many teenagers, my social life was my whole life and I daydreamed of being rich and famous someday. I saw how hard my parents worked but that seemed so far away from my daydreams. I may not have been paying much attention in those days, but somehow their work ethic became instilled in me.

During high school I worked for my parents in the string of retail stores they owned. I never considered retail as a career; it was just something my parents made me do. They also insisted I go to college. Resistant upon arrival, it took about five minutes before I was so glad to be on my own. I was 17, on my own and I never moved back home.

My parents were not able to save any money, so I put myself through school with student loans and restaurant jobs. I was the first in my family to graduate from college with a pair of proud parents to cheer me on. Armed with a liberal arts degree and five years of acquired skills in the restaurant industry, it took me eleven years to pay off my loans. During that time I worked as a teacher, a social worker, a waitress and a bartender.

Not long ago I asked my parents what they wanted to be when they grew up. They both said they didn't know. They are only in their 70's so they have time.

The way I feel about that question now is that there really is nothing to be. The fact that we are so focused on having to "be somebody" shows what we value in our culture and how much we limit ourselves.

I never had an answer to this question. I never knew what I wanted to be when I "grew up." There are some people who know from an early age what they want to be and they go for it.

I think that inherently we all want the same thing out of life. We want to be loved. To feel safe and secure. We want to be happy so we spend a lot of time pursuing things that we think will accomplish happy. That's really it. The rest is all one long strange trip.

If I had it to do over again I think I might have gone to Medical School and become a doctor. It's important to use your smarts to make a good living so you may have the freedom to pursue your happiness.

What do you do today to make a living?

I have been really fortunate. I do a little bit of a few different things. I just sold my coffee house that I ran for six years so I am in a transitional period. I manage my family's income property, co-manage a Charter Fishing business with my partner who is a seasonal fisherman and I build and maintain websites. I have always seemed to be able to make a decent living, travel a lot and not be tied down to a 9 to 5 schedule. I work mostly in the summer and take most of the winters off.

Describe the worst moment of failure in your creative/ entrepreneurial career.

Honestly, nothing really comes to mind. I pretty much do anything I decide to do. By the time I would have gotten too scared to do something, I've already tried it. My failures have come from not sticking to any one thing and following it through. I get mired in details and try to do too many things. In some cases I will never know how far I could have taken myself if I had just stuck to the process in one area.

Describe the best success you've experienced in your field.

Buying a coffee house, building up the business and turning it over for a good profit would be considered a success.

When my partner and I purchased the business it was just fledging. We worked as a team – he with the vision and ability to get things done and me with the detail oriented ability to sustain daily operations and carry out the vision – we make a good team. The business flourished under our close supervision. We sold it as a stepping-stone to create another business project. Armed with some cash and six years of experience, we are currently getting ready to begin the next project.

Do you feel there is a connection?

Through the coffee house experience I gained a lot of knowledge about what it means to be be an "owner" vs. and "employee." Having to manage a staff has taught me so much about myself. Working closely with a partner who had opposite strengths and weaknesses has helped me identify my strengths and weaknesses. I had to learn how to give up control. The most important thing I learned was how important it is to surround yourself with people who know more than you and trust them to help you get done what you cannot. All entrepreneurs are aware of their strengths and weaknesses and become successful by knowing how to put together the best teams.

Did you ever think of quitting or giving up, and more importantly why did you keep going?

Honestly I feel as though I am just getting going. If I had known the challenges I was to face before going into most things I've done, I would have been too afraid to try.

For instance when I was really young I wanted to be a musician. I wanted to play guitar like my dad and brother but girls didn't play guitar. Finally, at 30, I stopped buying into the fear driven myths of life and I learned to play the guitar. I wrote songs, cut records, put together a band and even did some touring. If I had listened to people that say "you can't sing" or "it takes years to be able to sing and play" or "you can't write songs with crazy chord changes" then I never would have done any of it.

"I have long since realized that dreaming of fame is the dream of a person who is unsure of herself. Now I dream of anonymity."

The truth is I'm not the best singer or the greatest guitar player. My strength was in the songwriting. I found that I love to write. It doesn't matter much to me now whether I am writing a letter, website copy or answers to these questions, it's all writing isn't it! I have long since realized that dreaming of fame is the dream of a person who is unsure of herself. Now I dream of anonymity.

In this crazy world, what is your best advice for a budding entrepreneur, artist, or innovator?

Don't assume that just because you are good at your art or your product that it will sell itself. If you are an artist, get good at managing your art "business" or your music "business" or your coffee "business." You have to create your own "buzz."

You can't be all things to all people so choosing a niche and getting really proficient in that area is a good idea.

Don't listen to anyone who criticizes your process unless they are coming from a perspective of experience in that process.

Be kind and treat everyone with respect.

Surround yourself with people that are good for you; you will know who they are.

Never stop studying and learning.

Hang out with kids as much as possible. They are energetic, authentic and not jaded. They are good for you.

Don't be afraid to be yourself. Always.

And most of all–don't take yourself too seriously. Have some fun!

Jeep Ward

DJ, TURNTABLIST, RECORD LABEL MANAGER

"As of now, I am actually quite unsure what I want to be when I grow up; my vision of the future is not necessarily based on a job or vocation..."

My friend Brian was DJing at Legion in Brooklyn, which has been an unlikely but frequent place for introductions. Jeep was trading sets with him, DJing some old-school hip-hop and hits of the 80s and 90s which hit home with me.

During a break I was hanging out with the smokers, even though I don't smoke. It was an excuse to step outside and chat with everyone. Turned out Jeep knew something of my home state of Maine, and we had a mutual friend in Sage Francis. We kicked into high-gear banter mode right away, and decided then and there that we'd consider a collaboration with music, art or business.

I attended several of his events, and he featured me on WPKN's "Jeep Ward Behind the Board" radio show. Our plan was to build a DJ set with live vocals. He was set to move to California, not long after, and the plan was put on pause, but he has helped me immensely with conceptualizing the tour for this book.

You'll see, as I did, that Jeep is a friendly Jack of All Trades, and it's great to have a talented friend who can talk business, music, radio and design. He was a shoo-in for an interview. I had a feeling there would be stories to tell, and I couldn't be more happy with the results.

~

What was your first job ever?

My first job ever was as a landscaper at the age of eleven or twelve. I put flyers in mailboxes around my neighborhood to cut lawns and it sprouted (hahaha) into a business, "Not Just Lawns Any Mower". Pretty quickly, I was taking care of 20+ lawns in my town as well as friends' parents yard work and handiwork. It intensified once my father became a realtor and was writing me into contracts of houses he sold as well. So by the time I was 15, I was working every weekend in spring and everyday all summer doing landscaping/painting/minor construction and making about $200 a day for about 3-4 sites per day.

Talk about how you felt after high school versus today on the question "what do you want to be when you grow up?"

When I graduated high school I had wanted to be a marine biologist but once I looked at the curriculums and saw all the work I would be doing outside of my field of study, I felt it would be too much. So, instead of pursuing this further I sort of arbitrarily picked Broadcast Radio to be my field of study, as I had started to be a DJ/Turntablist around age 17.

As of now, I am actually quite unsure what I want to be when I grow up; my vision of the future is not necessarily based on a job or vocation per se, but just allowing myself to create art and meet my basic needs of food & shelter.

Part of this consists of a plan to move off grid to grow and hunt most of my food while still being able to have time to make art (sonic, graphic, etc.). Outside of that, all I want to be able to do is have enough time outside of my means of support to create art/broadcast/podcast. If all those things ARE my means of support, great, but I won't die if it's not. I would continue these pursuits no matter what.

What do you do today to make a living?

I run a record label, Fake Four, Inc. & DJ (clubs, touring, bars, weddings, etc.).

Describe the worst moment of failure in your creative/entrepreneurial career.

I think the worst failure I ever suffered was two years ago I booked gig at Soda Bar in Brooklyn through a friend who was bar tending there and knew my work. I confirmed the gig about a month in advance with the manager, a Russian woman whose name escapes me now. So on the day of the event, I am on my way into BK from CT (where I live) and texted my friend Marco, to which he replies "Oh I don't bar tend on Saturdays anymore there", which gave me pause, but figured it would be fine, as I had confirmed with the bar manager, not just Marco.

I get there, get set up and the cross fader is dunzo...eh I'll just use the volumes instead no problem there. So I start rocking and by about 11-ish the back is pretty full and people are *dancing*, always a good sign as I have already launched into my electro stuff, as that's just where the set went. A bit early for it, but seemed to be working, so there it was. On top of that, at least five people have come up literally said, "WOW" and walked away, word.

So at about 12 the bar manager asked to speak to me outside which was strange, especially as I only had three minutes to talk. He launches into a soliloquy about what a terrible DJ I am and how they had to call one of their regular DJs to come in to take over, as I am just "killing the room with my shitty music"...huh? OK fine, I'll just get paid and leave, no problem here. So I get back in and close my laptop and start unplugging to which my peoples who came out say "What happened?" I tell them I am done for the evening and leaving. Immediately following this the 'Rescue DJ', who had oddly enough been there all night, comes up and tells me all that I was doing wrong and how she makes a living DJing and maybe someday I can be as good as her...WTF? After that, outside of the embarrassment of being cut mid-set in front of fans and friends, I was really shaken to my core about my skill. "Maybe I am a terrible DJ and people just won't tell me?" "Should I just quit now?" etc.

Describe the best success you've experienced in your field.

The best success I have ever had was when I was touring Europe in Winter, 2011. I was in Prague and I went on a walking tour during the day and met an Aussie named John Wilikins who turned out to be a rapper and was performing a few nights from then for Australia day at an Aussie hostel and bar. He asked if I wanted to run beats for him and I said sure, so I show up and he had already performed, but I had my laptop with me so he asked if I could DJ. Turns out the sound man knew me from doing gigs in NYC (small world!) and was more than happy to set me up. The club, not knowing me from Adam, was a bit nervous about what I would do so they said I had 30 min to rock. After about 10 min the bar was going ballistic and the manager asked me to DJ 'til close and offered to pay me 2,500 crowns, kroners, I don't remember the currency (exchange value was like $150). The bar was already pretty full from the Australia Day event, but I noticed a lot of people on their phones and in about 30-45 minutes it was wall to wall people until they cut sound about 2 hours later. It felt pretty amazing to walk into a spot in a foreign country, with not a person knowing who you are, get busy and really hold the crowd.

Is there a connection? If so, what is it?

I feel that both of those events really helped me to persevere in what I was doing as an artist. A lot of the time my eclecticism in so far as playlist and mix style is a bit jarring from other DJs, but in most cases people are just very taken by surprise.

As a result I see it as not going well, when in fact it is the opposite. The Prague gig really helped me to see how as long as I am doing what I do, not forcing songs or mixes, it will go well and entertain almost anyone.

Similarly, the FAIL gig was a sign that no matter what, you are going to have some *really* annoying politics to deal with in this business and people will be jealous and try to tell you things to make you quit. You just have to keep trying and doing what you know is right in your heart and it will resonate with someone, hopefully many someones, but it starts with one person mostly and not a friend or someone you are sleeping with either. A real fan who sees what you do and connects with it.

Both instances were examples of me being lauded and despised for being a bit different and choosing to re-contextualize familiar music to make it something different and original. I'm not reinventing the wheel, I just want to have a fun party that people will remember. Sometimes that means mashing up Black Moon with Thievery Corporation and some will be blown away, some will hate it. In either case you have made an impact.

Did you ever think of quitting or giving up, and more importantly why did you keep going?

I have and will continue to think about quitting ALL THE TIME; I think if you don't you aren't really pushing yourself to get beyond your comfort zone and do something amazing. Which it won't be at first, but after some work it can turn into that.

For the most part I keep doing this because A) I love it and B) I really don't know what else to do. I continually get wild hairs that I want to be a 9-5er and just get a paycheck and be done with it. Every time I do go out and get a job, I get pointed right back to being an artist—and pretty quickly too in most cases. Employers know when you don't give a damn no matter how solid your work ethic is; they want the job to be your life and for me it just isn't and never could be. So I'll either sustain, succeed or die. A bit grim, but it is the truth.

In this crazy world, what is your best advice for a budding entrepreneur, artist, or innovator?

Make sure you are wholly passionate about what you are pursuing, because like with my experience with employers, you def can't fake the funk when you are starting a business, struggling as an artist, innovating on idea X. A lot of blood, sweat and—yes—tears go into all of these pursuits and it's not a easy row to hoe. Many of your hours will not be recompensed, and in the beginning you will be paying out more than taking in and all that work doesn't always equal success either. Much of the time these ventures fail, horribly even—like wreck your credit for the rest of your life horribly; thankfully I have escaped this, but know others who were not so lucky.

This is the business model for any new venture though unless you have some significant start-up capital and even then it only means you'll be paid until the money dries up or the idea succeeds. So, if you are wanting something safe and easy, get a 9-5.

Chris Warren

MUSICIAN, RESEARCHER & "MAD SCIENTIST"

"I remember watching movies as a kid and always gravitating toward the mad scientist characters, like Doc Brown in Back to the Future."

For the life of me I can't recall why I was in the dance studio down the hall, but there I was. I had recently applied to go through the then-rigorous panel process for becoming an artist in residence at AS220. There were a few other people in the studio, including Chris. He and I got laughing. Perhaps this went differently than I remember, but we got on to some foolishness like somersaults or cartwheels, and in doing so, I ended up with a gash in my side from running into the fire extinguisher box.

He found me a bandage, and we ended up talking about what he did at the place, why he was there. He had a studio on the third floor, where I would eventually live too.

Chris is unnaturally smart, with a boyish sense of humor and a plain mid-western demeanor otherwise. We ended up working together on a lot of projects, including the formation of a 4-piece rock band, Reverser. It was good times.

Chris always had a pedal board or guitar that he was building or ripping apart, and spent a lot of time working on the conceptual side of audio, such as foley and sound design. It seemed only fitting when I heard that he was heading to California to pursue a second degree in the field of electronic music. There he developed all kinds of crazy and awesome devices and software... and somehow he started to eat sushi. I told him that the West Coast had really affected him.

I hope you enjoy the following interview. Chris is an unusual and fun person, and I'm honored to share his answers with you.

What was your first job ever?

First ever: crushing cardboard boxes and putting them into a dumpster behind a crappy mom and pop computer shop when I was in high school.

First in my field: Assistant engineer at a tiny recording studio.

Talk about how you felt after high school versus today on the question "what do you want to be when you grow up?"

I remember watching movies as a kid and always gravitating toward the mad scientist characters, like Doc Brown in Back to the Future. I love the scenes in his workshop where you can see all the odd gadgets he's cooking up. I've always been curious about this. Looking around my place right now, I see a disassembled player piano, half of several guitars, speakers of all different designs, and wires everywhere connecting it all. So I'd have to say little has changed.

What do you do today to make a living?

I play music, do audio research, and teach undergraduate classes in audio production.

Describe the worst moment of failure in your creative/ entrepreneurial career.

I used to own a recording studio. My partner and I worked at it nonstop for over two years. We put everything we had into it and tried really hard to make it work.

In the end, we tried too hard, never taking a day off, never having any downtime, so after two years we were so burned out that we couldn't go on. I had never experienced this before and didn't realized that burnout can be a huge risk when starting a company (especially a small one).

Describe the best success you've experienced in your field.

I'd say my career trajectory has been defined less by a single crowning achievement but more a continuous series of small successes. I've toured America playing music. I've travelled to Sweden to demonstrate my musical instruments. I've mixed albums I cherish. I picked up a master's degree along the way. I wrote and recorded an album of sonic hallucinations. I've been a part of several arts cooperatives. None of these is individually much to brag about, but my point is that perseverance has rewarded me with opportunities to do interesting things every day.

Is there a connection?

Closing down my recording studio was soul crushing at the time, but it propelled me on to the next thing. I learned that I could choose to look at an event like that as a failure (closing the studio) or a success (running a studio for two years and learning a lot in the process).

"...Perseverance has rewarded me with opportunities to do interesting things every day."

Did you ever think of quitting or giving up, and more importantly why did you keep going?

As frustrated as I've ever been, I've never felt any real temptation to give up, since in my mind this would mean walking away from all of the things that interest me. I keep going because this is what inspires me. Oh, and it also helps that I'm not very good at anything else...

In this crazy world, what is your best advice for a budding entrepreneur, artist, or innovator?

Do interesting things. Surround yourself with others who do interesting things. Engineer your life such that doing interesting things is the only option.

Sondra Woodruff

MUSICIAN, PERSONAL TRAINER

"My passion had left me with a broken heart. I tried to shut it out. But my soul wouldn't let me."

Sondra was, I thought, the coolest person I worked with. Every time I saw her she was smiling and, what's more, making other people smile. I also noticed she seemed calm when things were chaotic.

We worked in a crazy high volume retail environment, and there were a thousand things that could ruffle someone's composure—but not Sondra. It's easy to have bad habits in this line of work—the usual stuff like drinking, eating junk or take-out food, poor sleeping schedule and general unhealthiness. In total contrast, Sondra is fit as a fiddle... actually beyond fit. I thought, "who IS she?"

For the longest time, I had no idea what her real name was. We didn't work the same shift, and I wanted to reach out to her, so I looked her up online. There she goes by the stage name Jack Lucy by Sonji. You can imagine my confusion. Do I call her Jack? Lucy? Sonji? Eventually, I got up the courage to ask how she preferred to be addressed. Sondra was her name.

Once we got acquainted, I found that she has a warm and genuine personality and style. I invited her to be part of my fundraising campaign, and though she's busy, she generously helped out. Later, I stood in a packed room and watched her live show at the Bitter End, and it was fantastic... an eclectic and entertaining mix of original and cover songs. It was roots, and rock, pop and folk with a touch of R&B. Sometimes she shared the stage with a male vocalist, and they played off of each other well.

A while back, Sondra left retail and took the leap toward full time personal training. I really respected the decision. It takes guts to freelance and establish a clientele. Over all, it's impressive to see someone work two fairly different fields on a professional level. I think you'll see what I mean as you read on!

~

What was your first job ever?

Cashier at a local grocery store in Pittsburgh. Loved break time. Donuts and my mom would bring me a chicken sandwich and fries from Burger King. Well I guess that's why I double as a personal trainer now. Yum!

Talk about how you felt when you graduated high school versus how you feel now about the question "what do you want to be when you grow up?"

Wow! I was so confused when I graduated. Unfortunately, my family had a huge influence on my decision making which put a huge thorn in my dreams after high school. Although, from the outside it looked like I was pursuing my dreams of becoming a famous musician with loads of opportunities that most would die for. But on the inside my soul ached for the approval of my family concerning my dreams and sexuality. After high school that statement meant the world to me and now.

What do you do today to make a living?

Musician/Composer & Singer/Songwriter/Guitarist.

Describe the worst moment of failure in your creative/ entrepreneurial career.

The moment I realized that I didn't believe in myself. EPIC FAIL.

Describe the best success you've experienced in your field.

Touring with the Backstreet Boys in Germany in 2005. I was the opening act in 3 cities.

Also, scoring a 90 min documentary 2008–I never scored anything before I took that job. I explored the depths of my "Developmental Courage" on that one and it paid off. I picked up an entire portfolio of docs, commercials, indie films and corporate videos from that one documentary.

Recently, playing guitar for an Atlantic records artist. I've never just played guitar for anyone.

Did you ever think of quitting or giving up, and more importantly why did you keep going?

I always think of giving up and quitting. I did for 6 years in my heart. My passion had left me with a broken heart. I tried to shut it out. But my soul wouldn't let me. Neither would my friends.

In this crazy world, what is your best advice for a budding entrepreneur, artist, or innovator?

As cliché as this sounds. You have to believe in yourself. Nothing else matters. You will have failures that you'll learn from. Don't shy away from them. They are more important than your successes.

"I learned that courage was not the absence of fear, but the triumph over it. The brave man is not he who does not feel afraid, but he who conquers that fear."

–Nelson Mandela

More Information

About The Author

Serena Andrews is an independent musician, media artist and blogger. She was born and raised in Bangor, Maine, and went on to study vocal performance at the University of Maine, then film at Rhode Island College and New York Film Academy, as well as business at The Center For Women & Enterprise in Providence, RI. However, most of her experience came from working directly with artists and businesses the field over a period of 20 years.

She is the owner of Dream Siren (publishing), and Dream Siren Records, in New York, NY, and has distributed many digital releases worldwide.

She likes roller skating, coffee, tech, travel, unicorns & other such geekery.

About The Book

EPIC FAIL super win is Serena's very first book. It was conceived in the winter of 2012, spurred by her own failures and successes as an artist and entrepreneur. She is researching for a second book, and touring with EFSW during 2013-2014. The DIY-themed tour has received funding through fans and followers on the crowdfunding platform, Indiegogo.

The release of EFSW also marks the launch of the site **dreamsiren.com**, where Andrews will document the tour, and blog on life as a multidisciplinary creative with a focus on DIY, small business and technology.

Where To Order

Currently, the book is available digitally and in print at **dreamsiren.com/epic-fail-super-win**, where a list of stores carrying it will be updated regularly.

Connect With Serena Or Ask A Question

Email: **info@dreamsiren.com**

More About The People

There is an up-to-date list of links to each person in the book at **dreamsiren.com/epic-fail-super-win**.